The Rise of the Versatile

The Rise of the Versatile

Gay Male Sex Roles in Australia

Peter Di Sciascio

First edition self-published in 2020 by Peter Di Sciascio

An earlier version titled *Defining Gay Male Sex Roles* was published in 2018 on the Little Gay Blog at https://littlegayblog.com/gay-male-sex-roles/

All inquiries should be made to the author at pwds17@bigpond.com

Printed and bound in the USA by Amazon.com, Inc.
Type is Garamond 12 pt.
Cover design by Peter Di Sciascio
Cover image, *Coral Watercolor Background* by Piti Panyapat (Shutterstock)

Disclaimer: The material in this publication is of the nature of general comment only and does not represent professional advice. It is not intended to provide specific guidance for particular circumstances, and it should not be relied on as the basis for any decision to take action or not take action on any matter which it covers. Readers should obtain professional advice where appropriate, before making any such decision. To the maximum extent permitted by law, the author and publisher disclaim all responsibility and liability to any person, arising directly or indirectly from any person taking or not taking action based on the information in this publication.

ISBN: 978-0-646-81394-3

Table of Contents

Introduction

'Gay' has its beginnings as a culture for homosexual men and women in the USA in the mid-sixties. The Stonewall riots in 1969 heralded gay culture's first public outing. Gay encompasses not just homosexual attraction and sex, but the full spectrum of social and cultural life as well. For the first time homosexual men could be looked at and observed in non-sexual terms.

Since then gay culture has witnessed decriminalisation and the establishment of long-awaited freedoms in many parts of the world. Gay men can now develop new ways (our ways) of identifying and relating to each other. A unique culture and community is emerging which is to some extent free of the influence of the heterosexual world. This grand project to establish our own culture is still very much a work in progress. The time from the first emergences from oppression in the 1960s, to today, where almost complete freedom is available, is just over 50 years. For a minority to go from 'oppressed and invisible' to 'out and free' in 50 years is light speed. Development in that time is fast and history becomes compressed. The emerging culture is haphazardly put together or not put together at all. It is out of this disorganised environment that gay culture is forming.

The characteristics of gay sex roles came out of decades of systemic oppression by the heterosexual world. In some respects, gay sex is warped by those experiences. A connection was made between femininity and receptive anal sex. 'Masculine' men were assumed to be

1

the penetrator in gay sex and, in some places, at the same time considered to be straight. The view of gay anal sex was wrapped up in the ancient heterosexual male/female binary. We now know that more often than not, the Masc-Penetrator/Fem-Receptive paradigm doesn't apply, that's if the men follow what comes naturally to them rather than what is prescribed for them by some outside force.

In recent times the presence of large numbers of out and free gay men has allowed extensive experimentation with gay sex, like never before in the history of mankind. New freedoms have allowed gay sex to emerge as an increasingly unique sex, more likely to represent its participants' desires than not. This transformation has accelerated in this century, the change being so fast that for many it has gone unnoticed.

Methodology

To try and understand these changes I will present observations, consider human history, biology and evolution, and add a dose of logical thinking and common sense. I will apply these to current day manifestations of gay male sex, in particular, sex roles, which are also known as sex positions or anal sex roles. For references pre-1960 I will use the word homosexual reminding us that 'gay' didn't start until the mid 1960s. I believe that reminders of history are sorely needed.

I am writing this from an observation point of Melbourne in Australia. I describe a theory; specific research has not been done. In fact, a significant problem for the gay world is that very little research has been done into gay life, sociology, sex, culture, etc. In many ways we are doing it 'on the fly' in unorthodox ways which, while in the absence of scientific research, is at least giving us something to work from. Speed is of the essence as the largest ever population of out and free gay men to ever be on this planet struggles to find its cultural footing.

The reader is reminded of genetic variation:

The evolutionary process for all living things, produces inherited errors and alterations (commonly caused by mutations, gene flow or sex/genetic shuffling). These alterations may not be compatible with life (a cause of miscarriages for example); they may present some desirable but not essential function or phenotypic characteristic, or be harmless but give no advantage. Often enough, though, advantage is gained, reproduction of the advantaged individual is favoured and over time the genetic 'accident' can become the norm. This forms one of the principles of evolution, that of natural selection.

At any point in time we can see the results of natural selection in the variations evident in humans. Core characteristics that are essential or highly desirable may be relatively stable, other characteristics may present as a spectrum of variation from one extreme to the other, e.g. from black to white, with grey in-between.

Observe the Population, not the Individual

T o make an observation about a spectrum of presentations, or a subset of that spectrum, I use the principle that the observation applies to the population not to the individual. Instead of thinking of someone who doesn't fit the observation, think instead about whether the observation is largely true for a population. Thus, the observational method allows for current genetic variations and the unique human ability to apply 'free will' to alter or override instinctual traits. It presents a population-view which is needed in this sort of study.

A primary focus of this book is to understand the presentation and influence of the strong human sexual forces of *Dominance* and *Submission* on gay male sexual practices and sex roles.

A method for reproduction has been instilled into all living things and is essentially instinctual; it can't be altered. Unique amongst animals, humans have the capacity to apply free will and can override or alter the outcome of instinctual behaviour. Human reproduction allows for the presence of instinctual and non-instinctual components. Reproduction can occur, as a minimum, using instinct only. Also, with the introduction of the contraceptive pill in 1960, sex and reproduction in humans can be de-linked, and we can have sex without reproduction in mind at all. This has resulted in a rethinking of the place of sex in human lives.

Once Upon a Time

Human sex has its origins in the beginnings of humankind. Perhaps we can imagine such early humans, with no language and limited intelligence. Instinct told the man that his penis needed to go into a woman's vagina. The male instinct is to spread his seed wide, minimising inbreeding and strengthening the gene pool. The woman's instinct is to control fertility and produce offspring.

To encourage the joining of males and females necessary to bring on reproduction, a few basic elements were put in place. Importantly, sex is made pleasurable for both parties and the male is made active. The best result is where only one party is active and instigates sex. Males produce endless numbers of sperm (approximately 40 - 900 million per ejaculation from puberty to death), and are the active partner. This is achieved with the addition of a good measure of the unique male sex drive and dominance. Women have limits on how many offspring they can produce. She has a limited period in her life when her reproductive system is active. The number of ova she carries is determined early in life and does not increase. For only a very short period of her menstrual cycle is the woman actually fertile. There are lengthy periods during pregnancy and childbirth where the woman is not fertile. Additionally, through the mothering instinct, the woman takes into account such things as her health, environmental conditions and safety in determining whether it is wise to get pregnant. It is estimated that the theoretical maximum number of births a woman could have in her lifetime is 26. Ideally reproductive sex need only occur 26 times, but human reproduction is not that ideal.

In theory, the man has an 'accelerator' on the amount of sex he desires because he has sex drive, and the woman has a 'brake', she doesn't have sex drive. Over time the success of the balance between the 'accelerator' and the 'brake' that would be occurring between men and women is very evident in the enormous growth of the human population.

At this point it is worth noting that if you bring two men together, instinctually they have two sex drive 'accelerators' and no 'brake'. This would largely account for the observation that gay men have significantly higher levels of sexual activity than heterosexual men.

In this model, the male's sex drive and his ability to have sex often and with multiple women, are far greater than those of women. A sort of 'scattergun' approach is in place with excess male sperm saturating the reproductive system compared to the available female ova. This ensures that female opportunities for reproduction are fully consumed and reproduction is maximised.

This begs the question; what happens to the inevitable unused sperm and absent sex events? If sex drive wasn't fully satisfied in males, then we can imagine the frustration, tension and potential for danger to both women and men. Early man, with limited intelligence and no language would not yet have devised masturbation as a solution. I believe that an instinctual solution was in place.

The Nipple Solution

The power of the male nipple; some readers will wonder what I mean, some will know very well what I mean. I refer to it as the potential in some men (approximately 50%, apparently random) for their nipples to be 'wired for pleasure'. Stimulating the nipple during sex can produce enormous sexual pleasure for the man and this can increase over time. Alas, some men's nipples don't seem to be wired at all, there being no obvious reason for the randomness.

In early times there was the potential for sexual tension to build up if male sex drive wasn't satisfied. This could result in fighting, violence and rape in what were pretty basic human conditions. While the penis is designed to be partly a sex organ, it is already wired for pleasure, the anus is not ostensibly designed for sex. I have noticed that while some gay men gain enormous pleasure from the sexual use of their anus, some do not, or at least gain very little. Today we might identify these men as Tops. Unfortunately, confirming my theory is made difficult with the Top's anus being one of the main battlefields in the war over sex roles.

I theorise that way back in time, natural selection (evolution) allowed a proportion of men's anuses to be wired for pleasure. Not dissimilar to the nipple, except this time not so random and with an obvious benefit. When necessary, community sexual tension could be released and excess sexual activity 'mopped up' by one man penetrating another man's anus. It may not be reproductive activity, but it feels great for both parties (assuming that the receptive participant's anus is wired for pleasure) and is an alternative when women are unavailable for sex. For this to work, not all anuses can be wired for pleasure (they couldn't all desire to be anally receptive at once, or nothing would get started). The penis is fundamentally wired for pleasure so in those men with an absence of anal pleasure (not wired for pleasure), the act of insertion of the penis into the anus of the other is incentivised. From that you can imagine the cascade effect.

I don't believe that sexuality is a determinant in the eroticisation of the male anus. From a biological and evolutionary standpoint, all men should have the potential I described above. We hear about heterosexual men 'discovering their arse' these days. I have had numerous encounters with men who wanted anal sex but were not attracted to other men. They thought they were bisexual; I think they are heterosexual with an anus wired for pleasure that they have just discovered. At the end of the day they still want sex with women, that's where their desires are oriented, the vagina being their objectified hole.

The feelings and sensations of dominance and submission are strong erotic drivers and sexual arousal stimuli in humans. They probably developed in early humans because they augment and facilitate the active and passive roles of men and women during sex ensuring that the sex happens without chaos or harm and that the possibility of successful reproduction is maximised. Such roles bring forth and encourage the necessary physical coupling needed for reproduction. Recent studies have shown a link between human arousal by dominance/submission, and increased reproductive success. It is hard to change such a clear instinctual desire as that. An instinctual thought or feeling, however, lends itself to much interpretation. Thus, it is with dominance and submission. They are strong instinctual forces; forever present in us, but forces that modern humans have 'fiddled with' extensively.

Human sex and reproduction have two components. There is the instinctual component (nature) and the learned component (nurture).

The instinctual component has the basic building blocks for reproduction. Humans can think and have free will when it comes to whether instinct is followed or not. There is the potential that if enough humans decided to ignore their reproductive instincts, the species could be threatened. The learned component mitigates that by making sex very pleasurable. Examples of instinct at work might be the presence of male sex drive, or the male's urge to thrust during sex. Some examples of learned sex might include things like the use of leather in sex as an erotic turn on, or the development of methods for group sex.

What about Gay Men?

The stage has now been set for a discussion of how the above applies to male on male sex in modern times. It is instructive to keep in mind that it is only quite recently that gay men have been free enough to start developing a culture, including a sexual culture, of their own. The sexual culture includes aspects that are intrinsic and instinctual, as well as learned and cultural aspects. Wanting to put a penis into a hole and thrust is fairly instinctual. Which hole, the different styles of thrusting, accuracy and skill, are largely learned. Both nature and nurture influence modern sexual activities with the nurture components generally being more visible. Unlike other living things we have free will, we can decide to ignore nature and instinct, but I believe that our underlying instinctual desires stay with nature even if we don't act them out. The development of human intelligence does mean that we are now more able to use our free will and make sexual choices rather than following instinct. But the instinctual ways will always be there until evolution and natural selection 'wash' them out (not in our lifetimes).

In this book I will concentrate on the characteristics of gay men's sexual practices that are largely determined or influenced by nature (not nurture) and use them to illuminate the emerging gay sexual culture and understand the current teething problems. To discuss the influence of nurture would be another book altogether.

Top, Bottom: Words of Confusion

T he words Top and Bottom make obvious reference to the sexual binary. They are thought to have originated in the US homosexual leather culture of the 1950s and the BDSM culture of the 1960s, and that they signified both a sexual and power binary. In the 1970s and 1980s the terms evolved as they were adopted by the gay community where they most often refer to anal sex positions The history is sketchy, like so much of our past we were not permitted to record our history, even if we were collectivised enough to see the need to record it. We weren't allowed to gather, or form groups where a commonality of experiences and knowledge may have created some history. Top and Bottom soon became a quick way of communicating whose dick went into whose hole; very handy at an anonymous meet in a park at night.

At that time gay sex was very much piecemeal, clandestine and focussed on anal sex. There would have been few opportunities to form relationships with other men and develop a more holistic sex life as part of a relationship. Cocksucking, for example, may have been the full extent of a gay man's sexual experience. Sex in a house, in a bedroom, in a bed, with a light on, was unusual. Think about why gay men like sex at beats, in unusual places, anonymous, and in the dark. So much of their current sexual behaviour, the learned part, is linked to their history. Meanwhile the instinctual parts that nature has given us, which are often the foundations of our desired sexual expression, rather than being learned and created, are actually now being revealed.

In modern times and with modern freedoms we are seeing for the first time what was always there.

Like all humans, gay men's sexual desires are greatly influenced by the traits of dominance and submission. Remove sexual interaction with women, and the need to procreate from the picture, and we see the unmodulated influence of these two strong forces. Using terminology from the 1960s, Tops are dominant and Bottoms are submissive. If you think about the desired sexual practices of Tops and Bottoms, they fit the binary picture of dominance and submission respectively.

In gay men these traits would be amplified by the essentially male level of sex drive and the amount of sex that was occurring where these characteristics are reinforced by the equally driven man with the complimentary role. The best way to see male behaviour in its purest form is to observe it when two men are interacting, and the behaviour is 'doubled'.

Back in the 1960s this binary concept of Top and Bottom was confirmed by observing that in sex a man either topped or bottomed, not dissimilar to the heterosexual model. Thus, in their naivety, a huge mistake was made (more about this later).

Reminder: Observe the population, not the individual.

You may be wondering that if some gay men are naturally dominant, and some naturally submissive, then why are all heterosexual men dominant with respect to women? While I have not set out to examine heterosexual male behaviours, the answer to this question would help illuminate gay male behaviour. That amongst gay men some may be submissive and others dominant tells us that these characteristics are not sex-linked. Men are not always the dominant party. It would be the same with heterosexual men, a proportion of heterosexual men do indeed carry innate submissive desires. Perhaps they would have benefitted from them as Early Man when they were the receptive partner in a man on man sex encounter. Yet, they then had to get up and seek women in an active and dominant way. What you see may not be what you get.

I do not believe that the presence of significant submissive sexual traits amongst gay men (along with dominance this is a binary characteristic), would exist only within the homosexual population (a unary characteristic). So much is possible with genetics but this seems unlikely. I surmise that the desire for sexual submission is present in some heterosexual men as well. However, it is not amplified by the high levels of opportunity and regular experience of the learned components as we see in homosexual men.

While it might enter the sex lives of some couples, the woman's desires, the couple's combined level of sex drive, and the negative influence of culture and taboo along with the presence of masturbation, would dampen its practice. In theory the heterosexual male is satisfied by the prevalent modes of interaction with women and would not seek alternate roles. While I believe that an individual's desire to be sexually dominant or submissive is determined by nature, I speak for men when I say that these roles are not essential for sex. While the mechanics of sex can often proceed without dominance or submission, they play a big part in opportunity, desire, passion and enjoyment.

The Mistake Revealed

Getting back to our huge mistake; what we did was create categories for Tops and Bottoms but no one else. Versatile men missed out. Versatile men naturally have a mixture of both dominance and submission as erotic drivers. This allows them to express themselves sexually with the ways normally associated with both Bottoms and Tops. Indeed, at any point in time, depending on what they were doing, they may have appeared to be a Top or Bottom by omission or commission and so were not appropriately recognised. The fleeting anonymous sex that was common at the time, didn't allow for a Versatile man to be seen flipping, so his versatility remained a mystery. These were not university graduates; they were most likely ordinary working men. The concept of versatility in sex was virtually unknown. Men of the time are sometimes maligned for introducing a troublesome heteronormative binary system. On the contrary, I think they did a sensational job with virtually no knowledge and in an environment where their sexual activities were dangerous and illegal. That Versatiles were banished to the wilderness for several decades is not the fault of these men, but of the oppressors.

Essentially, Versatile men had to identify with one of two categories already established, straight jacketing them into roles that were not totally natural for them. In fact, definitions and roles *per se* grate against the fundamentals of versatility. The mistake occurred because at the time there was so little knowledge about gay sex. They were not allowed to study it, record it, or spread the word. The heterosexual model that was used as a comparator was not entirely helpful; **there is no versatility in heterosexual sex**. For versatility in sex you need same-same, both parties require the same 'bits'. They looked at the heterosexual model and missed that one. Oops!

There was constant dissatisfaction with the fixed roles, rules and agenda applied to sex. The now emblematic expression "go with the flow" was often heard from those who were disaffected. That expression is anathema to Tops and Bottoms and its presence can still be used as a marker of a Versatile man's profile in an online meeting app. Of course, the dissatisfaction seen at the time was from the Versatile men, stuck in the binary sex world that had been created, but they knew no better.

Rarely is something completely black and white in nature. As long as it is compatible with life there will usually be black and white, and a grey scale in-between. The grey appearing over time with genetic variation. The expression of the characteristic (black-grey-white) will be 100% (black or white) at the extremes, with a graded mixture of the two in-between (grey). Tops have the characteristic of 100% dominance influencing their sexual activities. Bottoms have a 100% submission driver. The long forgotten Versatile men have dominance and submission mixed to varying degrees to produce a group with a spectrum of sexual and erotic drivers and behaviours.

There were no significant numbers of gay men identifying as Versatile until about the mid 1990s. Their numbers have since exploded such that they are by far the largest group. Those left in the Top and Bottom groups are genuinely from the extremes and may exhibit sex with the maximum and purest influence of either dominance or submission, never changing to the other which they genuinely don't understand.

A Not-exactly-scientific Experiment

Wh

hen I have a Top or Bottom or Versatile friend visiting, it's not uncommon to be asked if there are any interesting Tops or whatever in my locality. I'm a Top, I almost exclusively interact sexually with Bottoms, so I might know the local Bottoms. Generally, though, Tops don't talk to each other, and relations with Versatiles are currently a bit strained. So I don't really know these other groups. I do a lot of surfing and cruising on apps like SCRUFF (Perry Street Software, Inc.). As I check out a profile, I put a copy of it into a 'favourites' folder labelled with one of: Bottom, Bottom Vers, Versatile, Top Vers or Top (that's if the profile identifies the guy's desired role or position, as the vast majority do). My thinking was that I could just hand my iPad to my visitor and open the relevant Scruff favourites folder for them to look at.

A favourites folder on Scruff has a limit of 250 profiles. Reach that number and you have to create another folder. In late 2017 I noticed something interesting about the order that the folders were filling. I then asked quite a few of my friends which folder do they think filled first? Only one got it right. The rest said Bottom or Bottom Vers. The answer is Versatile (what I often refer to as Fully Vers). This unintended research is not highly scientific, but the numbers are big enough that they are certainly indicative of the population.

As I write: Bottom –   folder 7
              Bttm Vers -   folder 4
              Versatile -   folder 12
              Top Vers -   folder 3
              Top -   folder 6

Many have immediately wondered about all the Bottoms who are contaminating the Bottom Vers group, yeah, yeah, yeah, heard it all before! The stats are hardly significant enough to support such speculation.

It's the significance of 12 folders of Versatile guys that should grab you, and the combined Versatile group being 19 folders. That's the story being told.

According to these data the commonly held view that everyone has become a Bottom is fiction. We are not seeing the wood for the trees, at least according to how guys identify on Scruff. Scruff is by far the most popular app in Melbourne and has great coverage; I think the numbers are a good indication of what is happening. There being no other data.

If we go back to the graded scale between dominance and submission, then the picture probably fits the reality. The Versatile groups should have the most numbers. Nature wants the 100% dominance and 100% submission points to complete the scale, that's typical for nature and is after all that's where it all started. In the case of this sexual driver, to get the 100% extremes there can be no versatility within them. If you add any versatility, then you don't have expression of the 100% extreme. There is a tipping point where the gradually decreasing amount of the opposing characteristic has to disappear. At the extremes either dominance or submission exist at full strength, dramatically influencing the desired sex. Desired sex on either side of the tipping point is so different that satisfying sex across the tipping point can be hard to achieve. This is the territory of Tops and Bottoms. Originally the words Top and Bottom were only applied to identify the insertive or receptive partner in anal sex, since at the time anal sex might have been the only sex happening. Now these words describe a holistic sexual practice informed by one of dominance or submission and devoid of desired versatility.

Generally speaking, Tops want to fuck, dominate, be in charge, control, teach, lead, compete with other Tops, focus on their cock and the Bottom's arse, plan and lead sex, lead the role play and mind sex and generally apply their dominant role to all sexual activities. Control is very important. Tops don't like surprises (surprises are uncontrolled) and they don't have many fantasies (it's hard to fantasise in a head that is such a controlled environment). The expression of these traits is desired and they are important for arousal. Some can be so important that their absence can prevent arousal. Interestingly the Top's arse is seldom used. He has no real desire there and he derives little or no sexual pleasure from it. Does that sound familiar?

The Bottom wants to submit. He loves to be the receptacle for pleasure and hand over all control, be fucked by multiple Tops and have all focus on his arse, which is highly wired for pleasure. In the heat of the moment even the most sensible and politically correct Bottom can tell the Top he wants to be treated like a whore and will ask to be raped. Their submissive drivers leave them with little control, the Top desires and takes all control, and hopefully he uses it wisely in these circumstances. The Bottom is highly susceptible to role-play and mind sex, and naturally desires the passive or submissive role in all sexual activities. Once he trusts the Top his submission can be complete. Bottoms love surprises and produce a constant stream of fantasies from a mind that has been freed of responsibilities and the cares of the world. A friend referred to them as 'fantasy factories'. At the end of the day though, the Bottom is still in control because he controls consent.

So, the Bottom Doesn't Lose Control After All

Of course, there may be variations in the presentation of Tops and Bottoms, largely due to environmental and cultural influences and the application of free will (nurture at work). Then there are the negative influences of decades of criminalisation and oppression (a sort of 'nurture' at work again). We should not forget or underestimate the damage that was done to generations of homosexual men and is still occurring here and in so many parts of the world.

I believe that what I have described are the fundamental sexual drivers for Tops and Bottoms. It is very defined and proscriptive, even the desire to define and proscribe comes naturally with a Top's sexual makeup. These gay men essentially have no desire to venture out of their patch. This is nature at work, not nurture.

The gay men in the now very large Versatile group are influenced by both dominance and submission to varying degrees. In the middle would be the fully Versatile men with equal measures of the two drivers. The result is that Versatile men have desires across the full range of gay sex activities. They like to be both the inserter and receiver with anal sex for example. Within a sex session they may change sides several times, referred to as flipping. Dominance and submission influence their desires and how they play them out, but the influences are not as obvious as with Tops and Bottoms. The extremes of such desires are usually not there, there is no 100% of either driver, always a mix of influences. Versatile men inherently don't like structure and fixed roles in sex, if these were present you could not have versatility. "Go with the flow" is the order of the day. I believe that there is a depth and intensity in Top/Bottom sex that just isn't present with Versatile sex. There is a sense that Versatile sex is 'paper thin' with the watered-down influence of dominance and submission, and that they will deliver whatever you want.

Perhaps this 'we can please everyone' attitude can be summed up in the lyrics of the song from the 1959 Hollywood musical Gypsy entitled Let Me Entertain You. Well ahead of her time, Sandra Church sings:

Let me entertain you
Let me make you smile
Let me do a few tricks
Some old and then some new tricks
I'm very versatile

Top and Bottom characteristics perfectly complement each other. Versatility doesn't exist for them and it is hard for them to compromise when having sex with a Versatile man. The very nature of versatility means the Versatile man is much more able to compromise and connect with a Top or Bottom. But it's by no means a perfect match. One can imagine how much compromise had to happen in the early days before Versatiles were recognised.

Reminder: Observe the population, not the individual. These lists are by no means exhaustive.

Key characteristics of Versatile sex:
- There is the desire to engage in both bottoming and topping.
- It is essentially democratic; all participants have equal standing and power.

- There isn't a role that is more vulnerable.
- Participants' desire that everyone experiences the sex equally.
- Participants are solo operators, they are independent.
- There is no driver for collaboration.
- No one is in charge.
- Sex is not planned, it flows intuitively.
- Versatility is ideal for threesomes and group sex.
- There are no fixed roles.
- All necessary body parts are wired for pleasure.
- There is no role play nor mind sex.
- No one has the teacher role.
- Versatiles can enjoy the full breadth of male on male sexual activities and experiences.
- There are no foci for innovation and excellence or pushing boundaries.
- There are no subgroups.
- Sex is fun, there can be laughter.
- Kink isn't emphasised, most kink operates with fixed roles.

Key characteristics of Top/Bottom sex:
- Roles are fixed, Tops always dominate, Bottoms always submit.
- Bottoms are naturally in the more vulnerable role.
- Sex is codified, it has rules and standards.
- The Top's orgasm is primary, the Bottom's is secondary.
- In sex the Bottom's cock is irrelevant as is the Top's arse.
- Sex is not democratic, there is a hierarchical disparity, Tops are on top.
- Sex is highly collaborative, Top and Bottom work together to achieve 'the very best sex'. Collaboration can be a key to satisfaction.
- Sex is serious but can be incredibly satisfying.

- Role-play is very effective. There is a strong psychological element to sex. There can be two layers of sex happening, that of the physical and the psychological.
- Sex is planned, managed and delivered by the Top.
- Tops teach Bottoms overtly. Bottoms teach Tops covertly.
- Tops discipline Bottoms (either verbally or physically), ensuring they comply with accepted behaviour and standards.
- Tops set the standards.
- There is an emphasis on innovation, excellence and pushing boundaries, it is common for Tops and Bottoms to specialise in a particular sexual activity and pursue excellence in that activity.
- There is no flipping. There is no desire to do the opposite activity at all.
- The Bottom expects the Top to deliver the Bottom's fantasies.
- Tops manage consent and safety.
- There is often an interest in Kink. Most kink is suited to a dominant/submissive environment.
- There are subgroups.
- Threesomes and group sex are difficult; one on one is most effective.
- Achieving total control and total submission in sex is prized.

Begin taking away items from either list and the respective sex starts to fall apart.

When reading these lists keep in mind my earlier comment, they apply to the population not the individual. There will be variations seen; however, I believe these lists are representative of a fairly pure presentation. I know from experience that some characteristics just do not crossover between Versatile and Top/Bottom sex. Some are so unique of the groups that they can almost be infallible markers. As mentioned earlier, sex between members of both groups inevitably involves compromise. My experience is that Versatile men carry the lion's share of the compromise, and Tops and Bottoms are the more dissatisfied with the resultant sex.

Two Types of Sex?

You will notice that I am now making reference to Top/Bottom sex and Versatile sex. I do this deliberately as I believe we now have two very different forms of gay sex happening. Unfortunately, they do not mix well. Traditionally, Tops have held the power in gay sex and gay culture. We now see that power shifting to Versatile men. I believe this is appropriate and Versatile sex should be the face of gay sex. Outsiders are unlikely to understand the complexities of Top/Bottom sex anyway. Versatile men have the numbers, they should be the biggest influence on the development of our nascent culture.

This power shift has led to some tension between Tops/Bottoms and Versatile men. Tops need to relinquish power; Versatile men need to use that power wisely. Older Versatile men were at one stage in either the Top or Bottom category, they have an understanding of Top/Bottom sex and the differences. Newer generations of Versatile men have often experienced no other type of sex than Versatile sex. They have little or no understanding of Top/Bottom sex and sadly my experience is they have little patience for it and don't take it seriously. I often interact with Versatile men who just can't understand or accept why I don't want to use my arse in sex. Too often this leads to quite unpleasant situations.

With regard to these internal tensions, the situation has become so unpleasant that a growing number of Tops have moved to a Bottom-only policy when hooking up for sex. There is such a rejection of not just Top/Bottom sex but also of the fundamental validity of Tops and Bottoms amongst gay men. Sadly, there is little understating of history. Much of what is being done to Tops and Bottoms by other gay men is not dissimilar to what gay men fought the heterosexual world over, in past decades. Being told by one young man that being a Top was 'just a choice' made me emotional because he just had no idea about what he had said. I hope that many of the readers can see the historical connections and human rights issues that triggered my emotion. I'm yet to see how we will get out of this situation.

The latest Versatile theory, coming out of the UK and being espoused in Australia is that Tops and Bottoms don't exist. They say that everyone is Versatile and to be a Top or Bottom is 'just a choice'. Modern homosexual man has adopted a way of having sex that meets our modern ideas of equality. Forgotten is that gay sex influenced by dominance/submission is instinctual for many men and to apply excessive pressure to them to conform with sexual equality is just another form of oppression. Apparently, every time I have sex with a Bottom and don't use his cock, I emasculate him (depriving a <u>man</u> of his role and identity). I'm selfish, I'm not really gay, I have restricted myself, I'm pathetic, I'm a Top because of a repressed memory of a childhood rape, Tops and Bottoms are dying out, and on four occasions I have had to tell a Versatile guy who has become horny for my arse that one more move and it's rape. Topping a Top seems to be quite an amusement for Versatile guys. These are just a few of my experiences. I don't see research being done here or in the UK to support or oppose the UK view. It appears that sociological research in Australia has to have a HIV/AIDS angle to get funding.

In the US the situation appears to be quite different. Top and Bottom sex roles seem to be firmly in place. It's Versatility that isn't treated seriously. It is sometimes thought of as 'a lifestyle choice for those in long term relationships'. I have no doubt that there are many Versatile men in the US, but the understanding of Versatility and use of the labels is quite poor. Academic research is being done and it appears that the funding does not have to be linked to HIV/AIDS, this is the country which had a poor response to the epidemic. Emblematic of this was President Reagan's inability to say the word AIDS until 4 years after the start of the epidemic. Much of the research looks at things like the incidence of Top and Bottom as it relates to the length of one of your fingers; that sort of thing. The fundamental flaw in much of the US research, as I see it, is that Versatility isn't included as a valid sex role. Often only Top and Bottom is researched. Instinct seems to rarely be considered.

Aren't We a Bit Late?

R esearch that might guide us on sex roles, versatility, culture, relationships, etc., hasn't happened and doesn't seem to be happening, but we need it NOW.

In 1978 Joseph Harry and William B. DeVall published a book; *The Social Organization of Gay Males*. It is based on data they collected themselves as well as from previous studies. The authors examined a range of issues of importance to gay men at the time.

Although they didn't use the word versatility, I believe they made the very first observation of versatility when they wrote: 'The majority of homosexuals appear to be flexible in their sexual activities and freely interchange sexual roles'. It took until the mid 1990s for Versatile men to identify themselves in any numbers.

Following are some examples of the topics that the authors covered:

- Mutual labelling – neutralising negative labels and reclaiming the words.

- Relationships among gay men – the first observations were made of the preponderance of open relationships amongst gay men and that these appeared to be more successful than those relationships with traditional fidelity. This wasn't revisited until the 1990s. They found that relationships were short lived, lasting on average three years, something that the gay community is only just starting to have a conversation about. Their data strongly suggested that attitudes transferred from the heterosexual culture are often ill-suited to workable interpersonal relationships between gay men.

- Adolescent experiences of coming out – The authors estimated the mean age of coming out to be 20.2 yrs and they found that the teenage years prior to this were often filled with turmoil. We still see the life and experiences of teenage gay men being controlled by heterosexuals. Is our community still afraid to reach out to the gay or questioning young men without the fear of being labelled paedophiles?

- Harry and DeVall also looked at what they called Gay Marriages. These were enduring homosexual relationships.

- They researched gay men's sex roles and considered them in terms of inserter/insertee, active/passive, dominant/submissive. Notably the words top, bottom or versatile were not used.

- Important issues about urbanisation and the development of homosexual communities are discussed. The concept of 'institutional completeness' is introduced as well as 'cultural impoverishment' and 'cultural completeness'.

- Sexual culture in the ageing is highlighted. We are only getting an identifiable elderly gay population now, for which we are ill-prepared. They noted the trend towards the acceptability of intergenerational relationships.

- The experience of gay men at work: discrimination and adaptation. Well before many countries had anti-discrimination laws.

This is the sort of research that should have informed both social theorists and those who make public policy. This is the sort of research that should have informed our developing community and culture. This is the sort of research that should have revealed those aspects of ourselves that were always hidden. This is the sort of research that would have facilitated an examination of gay male sex roles and a subsequent resolution based on fact, science and medicine rather than in an atmosphere devoid of the scientific method, analytical thought and compassion.

What happened to the work of Harry and DeVall, and the few other trail blazers of the time? I believe we can put it down to one word; AIDS. The AIDS epidemic was first detected amongst gay men in the US in 1981, not long after the book was published. In many western countries resources that might have been earmarked for the conduct of sociological research and to assist in timely formation of gay culture and society, was swiftly diverted, and necessarily so, to the battle with AIDS. In places like Australia, this diversion is still occurring. By now, gay men should have largely matured into their own culture and society. The presence of three sex roles should no longer be a point of debate and division. We should have a stable, rather than chaotic, environment to work through these issues.

The epidemic was not of our making. What I have described is yet another example of the 'collateral damage' that continues to plague gay men.

Everyone's a Bottom

A frequent catchcry for the Bottom-shamers and Bottom-haters is that 'everyone is a Bottom'. The implication is that the Bottoms are selfishly occupying the Tops and everyone else is missing out. Of course, that would have been said in more colourful and hateful language. I believe that recreational drugs do increase the desire and ability to use the arse sexually and decrease the abilities of the cock. But that's not the full picture. Who wants to bottom? Bottoms, Bottom Vers, Versatile, and Top Vers all want to bottom sometimes. That's a lot a gay men, almost everyone. They all want to be fucked at some frequency anyway, that frequency increases with the influence of recreational drugs. We are not seeing more Bottoms; we are seeing more gay men wanting to bottom more often. We should also remember that the capacity of the arse is significantly greater than that of the cock. In the marketplace, when it comes to fucking, one Top doesn't equal one Bottom.

Can We Fake it?

The question arises; can we change teams or fake it? For Versatile men who instinctually have desires across all roles and activities, it's hard for them to imagine that someone couldn't. Just like when I think of Versatile sex I shudder at its uncontrolled nature and wonder, 'who is in charge?' That is truly my first thought. Being in charge is an enormous erotic driver for Tops. Not having a sense of being in charge can negatively impact arousal.

For a Top or Bottom to fake it; to change and become Versatile, then they have to fundamentally change the way they use the cock and the arse. The cock is inherently wired for pleasure, that comes with being male. Bottoms often don't have a great desire to use their cock in sex. But they are men, they can be aroused and with practice they can fuck. With regard to the rest of being a Bottom, it's much harder to act against your desires. You can learn to do things, but that doesn't mean you desire them or enjoy them. Sex is supposed to be about enjoyment.

Using the arse is a different story. The arse is not ostensibly designed as a sex organ. Inherently it is not erotically wired unless you are one of the 'lucky' men. Without a significant sexual reward, it's not easy to stick something the wrong way up the arse. For this reason, Tops have a hard time being fucked. They usually don't get very good at it and never enjoy it. Dominance and submission, structured sex and fixed roles, for example, are instinctively so important for Tops and

Bottoms that outside of this paradigm it can be hard for them to get satisfying sex.

If they wanted to change and become a Top or Bottom, Versatile men have the advantage of been erotically wired and incentivised to have desires across all activities. What they really struggle with is the overt, intense and concentrated presence of dominance and submission, the use of role-play and generally the psychological aspect of sex. These can only come into play when roles are fixed and sex is structured (characteristics of Top/Bottom sex and not Versatile sex).

This inability, in my experience, does not worry them at all. I have concluded that this is the case because they don't even know that this layer of sex exists for Tops and Bottoms, let alone understand its importance to arousal and satisfying sex. It's likely that the psychological layer of sex is another thing at the tipping point of the scale that I mentioned earlier. It requires fixed roles and a hierarchical disparity, neither of which exist with Versatility. It is incompatible with Versatility and therefore is not a driver, or desired, by Versatile men. They can't conceive of it just as I can't conceive of how to be submissive. Also, rather than try and do activities that they don't desire, Versatile men, who change sides, have to resist activities that they do desire.

What's in a Verb?

At this point we should explore the difference between the noun and the verb. The nouns, Bottom and Top, have different usage than the verbs (to top, topping, to bottom, bottoming). The nouns describe the individuals and their roles in sex, the verbs describe the anal sex activities. It's a bit confusing but that's my interpretation of current usage. Online I say I want to meet Bottoms. I then have a constant stream of Bottom Vers and Versatile guys wanting to bottom for me. They mean they want to be fucked in the arse by a Top. I am however looking for the whole Bottom that I described earlier, his erotic buttons complement mine so it's inevitable I am more likely to get satisfying sex. This is no slight on the Versatile man. Ideally, we should drop the use of bottom and top as verbs and name the activities instead. I once heard this:

A Versatile man is never a Bottom.
A Versatile man is never a Top.
A Versatile man is always a Versatile man.
A Versatile man might fuck.
A versatile man might be fucked.
But he is never a Top or a Bottom, he is always a Versatile man.

The Future

In the future I hope that Top/Bottom sex and Versatile sex are accepted and that one is not seen as better than the other and that both are considered natural. Neither group should impose its sex upon the other. The newly empowered Versatile men need to accept that Tops and Bottoms are different because we are different. It's nature not nurture that underpins that difference. Bottoms have always been in a vulnerable position; their submissive role puts them there. It's where they find good sex. Fortunately, the Top's role, along with a strong driver for collaboration, protects the Bottom. Versatility does not naturally accommodate a weaker party; it assumes that all are equal. This especially has implications with kink and BDSM where care is needed as we are seeing safety compromised.

It is no accident that a Top is writing this. Traditionally Tops are the teachers and leaders. The sexual desires of Tops lead to structured sex, labelling, power, etc. Tops are well placed to recognise these characteristics and their influence. Also, Tops are more likely to spot the absence of these characteristics and the reason for the absence. Young Tops and Bottoms are still coming through the ranks. To be a Bottom so unfashionable these days, anyone saying he is a Bottom must be the real deal.

The embarrassing practice of Bottom shaming continues with Versatiles being the main source. This practice still references archaic heteronormativity that negatively links Bottoms with women and effeminacy.

Research is needed into the basis and nature of two ways of having sex appearing in a small population with the incidence of each type of sex being unequally split (currently looks like 70%/30%). Homosexuals have never been in this position before in history. Never before, in the history of mankind, have we had so many gay men in this place living a life that is out and free. It is only since about 2000 that we have arrived at this momentous position in Australia. We need to accept the possibility of fundamental change revealing itself, change that we can't control. We may discover things about ourselves that could not be seen in the past. With the freedom to follow our natural ways and sexual desires, have we uncovered something unique amongst human beings and other animals? What are, and what will be, the cultural implications? As a minority within a minority, how are Tops and Bottoms fairing at the moment? Do relevant health practitioners take into account that as gay men, Bottoms face the same stressors as their Top counterparts, but as Bottoms they encounter additional stress which is exacerbated by the fact that the oppressor is within their own community.

I suspect we are on very new ground and that these issues are not being properly studied. I haven't examined what is happening with the nurture or learned components of sex. That would be a book of its own.

A Final Note....

In this book I have described the typical features of three sex roles displayed by gay men. It is by no means meant to be proscriptive and it is based largely on observation. As I have mentioned throughout the book, it applies to the population, not the individual. There will be individuals who deviate from the typical, maybe because of culture, fashion or lack of knowledge. Maybe they are invoking free will. I have only really addressed the instinctual parts of sex. The influence of the learned or nurture component should not be underestimated. However, there seems to be a general reluctance to acknowledge that humans have instincts which date back to the very beginnings of humans. These instincts can pervade our behaviours such that we don't even recognise their influence. I believe that what we are seeing is the now out and free gay man's instinctual sex behaviour, previously hidden, but now being revealed. Current arguments about gay men's sex roles seem to assume that we can redesign and implement a sex system for modern times. I argue that there are fundamental aspects to sex, i.e. instincts, which cannot be changed and ultimately, we are happiest when we follow them. In addition, while the dominance/submission scale is a graded scale, there's no real crossing of the tipping points. We are either Versatile or Top, or Versatile or Bottom. If we are true to our instincts, we find that we can't change teams and at the same time enjoy satisfying sex.

To be true to his desires, a Versatile man must be versatile, as does a Top or Bottom man to his respective fixed roles. It's the next level that creates the challenge. Versatility presents constant sexual choices; Top/Bottom sex does not. This difference forms the main tension point between the two, as I see it today.

The Rise of the Versatile

Quora Answers

Quora's mission is to share and grow the world's knowledge. The heart of Quora is questions — questions that affect the world, questions that explain recent world events, questions that guide important life decisions, and questions that provide insights into why other people think differently.

I have written over 1000 answers, many in the gay sections of Quora. Following is a selection of those answers that relate to the subject matter in this book.

www.quora.com

This first answer isn't strictly related to the book. I have included it because, unexpectedly, it has by far become the most viewed of my answers with nearly 70,000 views.

Can straight men finger themselves?

29 October 2019

Of course, any man can finger himself if his hand can reach around to his anus. Just putting some fingers in is likely to be pleasant. Although, the hand will be curved to get into the anus, this is generally not comfortable. A proper fingering can be significantly more pleasant if done by someone else with skill. This can be by the man's partner, male or female.

In this answer the Top refers to the person giving the fingering. The Bottom is the person receiving the fingering.

The anus must be clean. The Bottom should have douched and washed.

The Top MUST trim and buff the fingernails of the hand that is to be used. Fingernails are the main cause of pain with fingering. Prepare all four fingernails, you may not yet know if you are likely to get to four fingers or not.

Make sure that personal lubricant and a towel are present close to the Top. The towel? I know what you are thinking.......most of the time it's just lubricant that you need to wipe up.

The best position is for the Bottom to be reclining in a bed. This allows for good eye contact between the Top and Bottom. You may need to put a pillow under the Bottom's hips to raise the anus. Don't forget that the Top should be comfortable as well. You don't want the Top to end up with an ergonomic injury. The next best position is for the Bottom to be on all fours, 'doggy style'. Certainly, the fingering is much easier, but I believe that the loss of eye contact is a problem.

Check your hand for cuts and abrasions, if present do not proceed. If you have to wear gloves then it's just not worth doing.

Be generous with the lubricant. I find that water-based lubricant is best as it's nice and slippery. Cover the fingers, hand and anus. Note that in this process both hands will get lubricant on them which can restrict what the Top touches, for example the phone or a drink.

Ensure you have consent to do the fingering but try not to have that qualified by the number of fingers. Let how far you get in be a surprise.

The Top should be positioned in line with the Bottom's spine and facing the anus. The fingers should be going in straight on. Unfortunately, the fingering can become uncomfortable and ineffective if the Top does not maintain this position, for example by leaning forward to kiss the Bottom.

Talk the Bottom into relaxing, and importantly 'allowing it to happen'. Tension in the sphincters caused by the Bottom not being relaxed is probably the second most likely cause of pain and discomfort after the fingernails. Tell the Bottom "this should be very comfortable, if it isn't, or if there is pain, tell me". It helps the Bottom relax more if he knows he can stop the fingering and that he doesn't have to cope with discomfort.

I start with the index finger and move to the pinkie. The thumb stays out. I gently hold the finger against the closed hole, moving it with a ticking action. You will find that the hole will eventually just gradually open for you.

Most of the pleasure of a fingering comes from the action of the fingers against the anus, which is at the entry. The anus has two sphincters and there is a short space between them. If there is any pain it will be in the area of the first and second sphincter. Beyond that very little pain can be felt.

You will find that with a gentle push the finger will just slide all the way in. Once there, you can stimulate the prostate by moving your finger in the direction of the penis. You will feel a bit of a lump on the wall of the rectum. That is the prostate. You should treat it delicately. Do not poke the prostate with your finger. Carefully rub it with the pad of your finger against the lump. The pleasure for the Bottom is very strong, he will certainly be able to tell you if you are at the right spot.

With a gentle motion bring the finger almost out, then go back in, then out, etc. doing a half twist as you do this. THE PACE SHOULD BE NO MORE THAN THAT OF A RELAXING MASSAGE -this is one of the keys to success.

On the outward stroke, stop just before the fingernails enter the sphincter area. Then move back in. This just minimises any repeated discomfort from the hard nails against the sphincters.

When the anus feels relaxed, and on an outward stroke, slip the second finger in. You will find that you might have to almost completely come out to be able to add the next finger. As you re-enter you will have to slow down for a bit as the sphincter acclimatises to the extra thickness. When you scrunch the fingers together before entering, you should be able to cover one of the fingernails with the other finger. Therefore, only one nail is exposed, further minimising any discomfort at the sphincters.

One finger might be the best you can insert with a beginner. Two fingers should be comfortable for a Bottom who is experienced with anal sex. It is not common for a Bottom to get to three or four fingers. If they do it is often due to the skill of the Top. When you scrunch three fingers together (again try and hide a fingernail) you will see that it is not as comfortable for either of you. If you are able to slide nicely in and out with three fingers, then you are likely to be able to do four, by introducing the pinkie.

The Bottom will probably think that you are still at two fingers, the sensation he feels is very pleasant, but not accurate. When introducing finger three or four I will often ask "how's that, feeling good?". With that you can get confirmation that all is ok without giving away how many fingers you are up to. The reason I raise this is that many Bottoms have never been to three or four fingers. If they think about it they usually get nervous and tense up. If you tell them once you are there they are more likely to be pleased and relaxed.

You may not be able to apply the massage motion to the four fingers. The pleasure will come from the sphincters being stretched. At this point I usually tell the Bottom that we are at four. I also tap the arse cheek twice with my thumb and say: "thumb's out". It is important to quickly reassure the Bottom that you are not going to introduce any more to the anus without their consent.

In theory you should be able to push the four fingers in as far as the big knuckles of the hand. This stretches the sphincters. Make sure you go in very slowly. You might be surprised how much pressure you have to apply when pushing the fingers in. It's ok, just keep checking with the Bottom. You may not get to the knuckles. At the Bottom's limit, hold the hand there. Only do the massaging motion if the four fingers move in and out comfortably, which is not common.

If you have got far enough in, the fingertips should be able to touch the wall of the rectum, which will usually feel mushy or maybe a bit harder.

While keeping the hand still, swirl the fingertips slowly against the rectal wall. This excites some very unique nerve endings and the Bottom should get a very strong pleasant sensation. Ask the Bottom to describe the pleasure and he will not be able to find the words for it. We can only feel it in these circumstances, and it has never been named.

You will find that most Bottoms have never been to four fingers or felt the pleasure of the rectal wall. Getting them there may be a significant event. Note, if the anus is a bit tight, you might find your fingers are being crushed by the sphincters, this could dictate when the fingering ends.

At any point the Top should be able to feel if there is any tightening of the sphincters. This is most certainly a sign of pain, tension or some other problem. If you feel it, stop and ask the Bottom what the problem is.

When you have had enough, it's time to come out. When coming out of the anus with anything (penis, fingers, toys, etc.) my rule is 'Always come out slowly, make every exit a pleasant one, and don't abandon the arse'. By abandoning the anus I mean that the Top's first urge is to run off and wash the lube off or start cleaning up, or something. Instead, for 30 seconds or so, give the anus some attention. Some tickling with the fingertips or gentle blowing on it. This is also the moment to lean forward and kiss the Bottom. Remember to hold your hands away.

Your Bottom should be relaxed, satisfied and impressed!

There are numerous sources of pleasure in the arse:
- the prostate,
- the rectal wall,
- the sphincters.

The three erotic sensations of the arse:
- stretch (of the sprinters),
- depth (a sense of getting further in),
- bulk (how much is in there).

Always try and stimulate a couple of those.

Your fingers should come out clean. If there is a small amount of soiling, dash off and clean it without embarrassing the Bottom. Remember to thoroughly clean the hand and anything it has touched, to minimise the chances of infection.

If you start giving these sorts of pleasures, you will have to accept the presence of faeces from time to time, and that you might be on the receiving end of smells and flatulence.

Is gay porn sexist? Why are Versatiles and Bottoms made to wear jockstraps or briefs, while Tops get to wear boxers or compression shorts with open flies?

7 May 2020

The wearing of those particular underwear is just to reinforce the roles of the participants. Jockstraps and briefs make the arse quite visible. Versatiles and Bottoms are supposed to be fucked in porn so it would be appropriate that the arse is visible.

Tops aren't fucked so to wear a jockstrap would expose their arse, which isn't appropriate. Boxers or shorts cover their arse. Tops are responsible for the fucking. It's their dick which is needed. Having open flies can expose the dick and make its use easy while the shorts are on.

Is there a gay male hierarchy?

4 May 2020

I don't believe that there is a gay male hierarchy in everyday life. We don't have families in the heterosexual style where there is a daily hierarchy, for example, with grandparents, then parents, then children by age. The strength of that hierarchy can vary with time and from one family to another. Gay men don't have this because we don't have traditional families.

Gay men haven't yet fully developed a culture and community. These are often places where you find some hierarchy (e.g. leaders), but we are yet to see what happens.

There is hierarchy with some gay sex. Versatile sex does not have any hierarchy, everyone is essentially equal. Top/Bottom sex, however, does contain a hierarchical disparity. An apparent power difference between Top and Bottom. This disparity is essential for Top/Bottom sex to work. Indeed, just as essential as it is for Versatile sex to not have any hierarchy. The effect of the disparity between Tops and Bottoms flows through in various guises to the range of subgroups. These subgroups being one of the many fruits of the disparity system.

Is it possible for a gay man to know if they are a Bottom or a Top if they have never had sex before?

1 May 2020

I believe it is possible for a gay man to know if they are a Bottom or a Top if they have never had sex before. I can describe my experience as a case in point.

It's a tragic matter of history that gay men have matured and blossomed sexually at a whole range of ages. The tragedy lies in the fact that many of these ages were unnatural, unhealthy and caused ongoing mental health issues. A gay man who is screwed over by sex is an all too common finding and something he is usually highly embarrassed about.

I came out as a gay man at the age of 30. Unfortunately, my coming out was not marked by a party but rather a nervous breakdown. At that stage I had no sexual experience with another person, male or female. Despite the sexually repressed world I lived in, and a complete lack of information, I still worked out that I was gay without any experience of sex at all, let alone with another man. I remember that when I came out I was very sure of that.

I don't recall exactly when, but my first sexual experience with a man occurred when I was about 32–34. I was a complete virgin until then. I remind you that there is a lot more to gay sex than anal sex. It was my late 30s before I had my first experience of anal sex, as a Top. Looking back at those early sexual experiences I can see the hallmarks of dominance (Top) despite the lack of experience of anal sex. Chiefly there was the urge to be on top sexually and to be in charge.

I now know that there are three sex roles in gay sex, a sex role being far more wholistic and complex than a sex position. The three are Top, Bottom and Versatile. Back then we only understood the first two. Our understanding of them was very much in terms of the two activities in anal sex. Now we know that these terms can describe not just anal sex, but a complex sex life informed by either dominance, submission or both.

At some stage I realised that I needed to engage in anal sex and adopt one of the terms to be gay. A not uncommon belief of the uninitiated at the time was that the older guys fucked the newbies. The thought terrified me. Inside I knew that I didn't want anything up my arse. At the suggestion of a gay friend, I bought some porn. That meant buying a VHS cassette by mail from the only territory in Australia that was permitted to sell such things. I also had to buy a VHS player. Fortunately I lived alone. I watched the porn and It was very clear who in the porn I wanted to be. It was the Top's role that I wanted. An added complication was that in stereotypical terms I did not look like a Top.

I was gay and a Top yet it was another few years before I 'topped' anyone. It was probably another 7 years, while in a relationship, that I 'bottomed' for the first time. That certainly confirmed my chosen path.

I believe that a gay man could know that they are a Top or Bottom if they had never had sex, but that this would only occur in pretty warped circumstances. Hopefully circumstances that don't occur anymore.

My story highlights some definitional issues. We are using the terms Top and Bottom differently now. Historically they referred to only the two activities in anal sex. Gay sex was really just anal sex in the past. It was only in about the 1960s-1970s that we were able to have sex in house, in a bedroom, in a bed, with a light on, without fear or harassment. This was a revolution for us. We discovered that we could have a more wholistic sex life and that we could get to know our sex partners and even have relationships. The terms Top and Bottom have changed meaning. They indicate a person's wholistic sexual practice informed by dominance or submission. That's the nouns. The verbs, to top, topping, to bottom, bottoming, refer to the activity of anal sex.

In the 1990s in Australia we saw the emergence of a group of gay men who identified as Versatile in sexual terms. They were neither Top nor Bottom. Their sexual activities and desires are informed by both dominance AND submission. Why they hadn't appeared before, is another story. In Melbourne, Versatile guys probably now constitute approximately 70% of the gay population. I'm not Versatile, but what if I was back when I was trying to work out whether I was a Top or Bottom. Wouldn't it have been better if anal sex was not the only marker. My point is that how we now think about these things comes out of pretty screwed up periods in history. So let's be kind to each other about this.

Unfortunately, the existence of these terms and their use has become a battle ground. The use of the words Top and Bottom comes out of a period where gay sex was mostly anal and in the park at night with total anonymity. Saying one of those two words could be a convenient way of negotiating sex. We now have more complex things to negotiate and to some extent those words fail us. Add Versatility to the mix, along with little understanding or research on these issues and the current battle between Top/Bottom and Versatile seems inevitable.

Do we need to have these terms, or similar terms? I believe that to some level we do. Unlike the heterosexual world we don't have easy recognition of potential sex partners. Gender doesn't help us, and we are in the minority amongst men. There is a saying that "a man is only straight when a gay man walks in the room". At this level, labels are important.

The next level is where the battle starts. Instinctively dominance is the driver for a Top, submission is the driver for Bottoms. Each desires to participate in their respective role, and not the other. Roles are fixed and sex is defined. Tops and Bottoms in sexual terms are perfect matches. In terms of what they desire to do, they see no choice, it is natural for them.

Versatile guys instinctively are influenced by both dominance and submission, although each at a lower level. This means that they desire to participate in the whole range of sexual activities. They can 'flip' from one role to the other. Sex is not fixed; in fact it is full of choices. Choices with Top/Bottom sex can mean chaos! Labels help Tops and Bottoms in their type of sex, they come naturally. Versatile guys don't need labels as they flip around all activities, they see labels as a negative constraint on them.

Sex between a Versatile guy and Top or Bottom is inevitably a compromise. Increasingly neither will make the compromise so we are seeing a separation occurring and the emergence of two types of gay sex. Considering that we have never been in this place before, i.e. we have a population of out and free gay men that is bigger than has ever existed in the history of all mankind. Perhaps what we are seeing with sex are things that were always there but that are only now being revealed. At this important time in our history we should not be surprised if nature throws up some challenges.

Is having to mostly always bottom for your significant other a bad thing when you rarely get to top because "I have to be in the mood for it"?

28 April 2020

It sounds like one of you might be Versatile and the other a Top. The Versatile guy who says he is always bottoming can do it and enjoy it, but every now and then he desires to top.

If his partner is a Top, then his reaction is exactly as I would expect. It's very controversial but I believe that Tops get little or no pleasure from their arse. The mechanism for this is unknown.

A match between a Top and a Versatile guy is neither a perfect match nor an example of incompatibility. Compromises will always have to be made. Eventually this damages the relationship. The solution I believe would be an open relationship where the Versatile guy could seek the company of another Versatile guys from time to time.

It would be easy to say that both are at fault here for not selecting fully compatible partners. But these matters are difficult to understand, they are not being properly researched and are currently a battle ground for the war that Versatile guys are waging against Tops and Bottoms.

How do male homosexuals decide who is the Top and Bottom?

28 April 2020

A gay man is a Top, or he is a Bottom, or he is Versatile. He doesn't actually decide which he is, he just is.

Remember that gay men's sex is usually much more than anal sex. For Tops and Bottoms deciding to do the other role can be very difficult. Just asking the question (are you Top or Bottom?) is all that is needed to anticipate their desired sexual activities or to not proceed if there is a mismatch. If you find out that the guy is Versatile then you may need another level of inquiry to be able to find out what they want to do.

It is inevitable that gay men have to talk about such matters almost immediately after meeting. There are three sex roles and some combinations are not compatible. To further complicate things, we are all men, visually we can't reliably determine who is Top, Bottom or Versatile, even if we have detected the gay man in a sea of straight men.

We just have to talk up front. Those that delay asking the question seem to be maintaining some sort of heterosexist romantic ideal. That just causes trouble.

Is the Bottom receiving and the Top giving?

24 April 2020

I'm a Top. My experience is that the Top is in the active role and the Bottom is in the passive role. For many Top/Bottom activities that appears to align with the concepts of giving and receiving.

The most erotic word for a Top is control, the more control he has in sex the more erotic he feels. The most erotic word for a Bottom is submission. Submitting takes the Bottom to a higher erotic plane. The two complement each other and they each have no desire to swap sides.

It's important to recognise that the receiver/passive/submissive role of the Bottom does not mean he doesn't do anything or has no power. Properly functioning Top/Bottom sex involves the Top trying to completely pleasure the Bottom. At the same time the Bottom is trying to completely pleasure the Top. How they do that is different because they have different roles. It is important to note that it can be quite an intense pleasure exchange, and that it is selfless.

There is a hierarchical disparity between the two. It's not abusive and Top/Bottom sex could not operate without it. In most of the physical sexual activities the Bottom is the receiver and the Top is the giver. In the psychological side of Top/Bottom sex it is the other way around. The act of submitting involves the Bottom giving control to the Top.

The Bottom is ultimately in control because he controls consent.

How can question of gender equality be reconciled when sexual relationships are not about men or women mating but about domination and submission?

22 January 2020

Mating is the purpose of reproduction. Nature instilled us with dominance or submission to help the coupling that needs to occur. Dominance or submission are in our genes, but they are not sex-linked. Sometimes the woman is dominant and the man submissive. Sometimes culture hides this from us.

Dominance and submission also flavour and inform other sexual activities, not just the reproductive act. I can't believe that nature made the dominant person abusive, and the submissive long suffering. Remember that a proportion of women are dominant.

The negative connotations that we have with the concept of submission were created by men and women. Chiefly to put women down or abuse them. Real submission without the negative interpretations is a highly erotic state for the person submitting.

Since the introduction of the contraceptive pill we have for the first time had a reliable method for delinking sex from reproduction. But sex has some instinctual components that we can't really change on a large scale. We can't reconcile gender equality in this case. Often biology doesn't withstand our equality tests. If you factor in that a proportion of submissive people are actually men, then I don't really understand how a gender equality reconciliation could be done.

Is it okay to be a Bottom? Are these sex role preferences in the gay community an issue?

22 January 2020

From my view in Australia, it's not ok to be a Bottom. Sex role preferences are an issue. I am speaking as a Top.

Bottoms are generally regarded here as low life sex scum. I don't know why, but those views come from Versatile guys. They are very critical of Tops and Bottom in lots of ways. They don't take us seriously because they don't believe we really exist. "It's just a choice" I am told.

In reality, two ways of having sex between men has developed. One reflecting the sexual ways of Versatile guys, the other brings together a Top and a Bottom in a perfect match. Most Tops treat Bottoms with respect. It is so unfashionable to be a Bottom these days that those that say they are a Bottom are the real deal. For me, knowing whether I have a Bottom, Bottom Vers or Versatile makes a huge difference to the way I have sex. I know which I prefer.

Versatile guys don't believe that it's ok to be a Bottom. The issue of Bottom, Top, Versatile in the gay community is not getting any better.

As a gay Bottom, how do I 'lie there and take it'?

6 Jan 2020

Your question could have several interpretations. I'll assume you are referring to receptive anal sex. By 'lie there and take it' I'll assume that you mean take anal sex that you don't want or that is not pleasant and that you want to know how take it without complaining.

Remember that there is much much more to being a Bottom than just anal sex. Explore some of these aspects of your sexual self through other sexual activities and role play. They may make you happier and enjoy anal sex more as you see it in the context of being a whole Bottom collaborating with a Top.

If you are not gaining pleasure from anal sex, or if it is uncomfortable, then find the confidence to tell the Top to stop or slow down. Communication is the key.

One of the most erotic states for a Bottom is submission. Are you getting to submission? If you are then to lie there and take it should be easier as it is inherently submissive.

Would humans continue to reproduce if sex was to be unpleasurable?

9 December 2020

This is an interesting question.

Human reproduction is driven by two components. Instinct and learned behaviour. The latter is where most of the pleasure comes in to play.

Humans are rather unique amongst animals in that we can think and have free will. We can decide not to follow instinct or to alter the outcome.

Reproduction is essential for the continuance of the species. Other animals just follow instinct and don't need incentives like pleasure. Humans can decide not to follow their reproductive instincts. If too many decided to do this, it could jeopardise reproduction for the species. At times when the number of humans was low this could have been an issue.

The way to ensure we didn't neglect reproduction was to add measures to reduce displeasure to the instinctual process and allow our imagination to assign all sorts of pleasures to the learned component.

If there was no pleasure, or if it was unpleasurable, I do think that many humans wouldn't do it.

Why do gay people have such a higher sex drive than heterosexuals?

13 November 2019

Gay people don't have higher sex drives than heterosexuals. What is causing your observation is that men have instinctual sex drive and women don't.

We all have within us the instincts required to reproduce without thinking or making decisions. Early man and woman had no language and were not intelligent. Reproduction went ahead purely on instinct, as it does for other animals. Man and woman didn't couple at that stage. Reproduction was required not just to increase the number of humans, but also to strengthen the gene pool. That meant that men would have sex with multiple women quite frequently.

What makes the man seek out a woman to have sex? He can't think it or learn it, so it's sex drive that makes him seek out a woman. Men have sex drive for this purpose. Men are the active partner in sex, so they are the drivers and initiators.

Women do not need sex drive in this scenario. They are passive and sex comes to them. In fact, if they had sex drive as well it would have made things difficult when they were both hunting for a sex partner. Women are not the active partner; the two roles need to be separate. Also, women have the role of nurturing babies and children. Not easily done if she is wandering around looking for men for sex.

We have come a long way. We can now think, we have knowledge, language, indeed we can even delink sex from reproduction with the contraceptive pill. But our instinctual sex drive is still with us. While we can modify the way it is expressed, it influences what we desire.

Think of a woman's lack of sex drive as a brake on sex. Men's sex drive is like an accelerator on sex. In a heterosexual relationship, what emerges as the relationship's sex drive would be a sort of average or compromise between the woman's brake and the man's accelerator. That final sex drive appears to be at the right level if the level of human reproduction is any gauge.

In very recent times we have finally seen the emergence of significant numbers of gay relationships, free and out. What we find is illuminating. Bring two men together and we essentially have two accelerators on sex. Each gay man would have a similar sex drive to a heterosexual man. It's the fact that it is 'doubled' and that there is no brake on it that causes the levels of sex we see in gay men.

Lesbians however appear to have quite low levels of sex in their relationships. They don't have the drive, effectively there are two brakes on sex.

As humans we can alter the expression of our instincts. More so than ever we feel we have disconnected ourselves from ancient instinct. So, if constrained, men might reduce their amount of sex. Similarly, women may increase the amount of sex they have because of social expectations or learned sex drive. But overall I believe that the above answers your question.

I have had people react in horror at the thought of women having no sex drive. I'm afraid the amount of sex you desire is not accountable to equality laws. I'm afraid that we cannot change our instinctual desires, only modify their expression. We need to accept that instinctual sex drive is just a functional part of reproduction. Nature never intended it to raise the status of men or imply women are less than fully human.

Is it true that 1 out of 10 people are homosexual?

23 October 2019

It is almost impossible to know. Remember that the word homosexual includes both men and women. The lived histories of lesbians and gay men are very different. We really don't know what the degree of visibility was at any point in history, so many hid in the closet or were otherwise invisible. So many never identified as homosexual (or whatever word was used at the time). We have no mechanism to count homosexuals now and there is no real data from the past.

Then there is the issue of geography. The situation varies so much from country to country that if we were to count homosexuals in one country we may never know if that count is representative of other countries. We could never even be sure of the accuracy in countries where homosexuals enjoy freedom.

Biology tells us that in theory the number of homosexuals as a proportion of the wider population should be about the same across the world now and in history. But many factors, not in the least centuries of oppression, make it difficult to imagine when we might have full visibility of all homosexuals in all countries. We could never be confident that we have got to that point. I'm in Australia, the scant population statistics we have only counted homosexual men in police records and HIV records. You can imagine that collecting population statistics on homosexuals will be greatly resisted.

I believe that the 10% you quote comes from some early research. I believe that sociologists and demographers now 'guess' that it might be something like 5%. That 'feels' about right but we will never know. Spending any more energy to improve the data will be a waste when the actual size of the homosexual population doesn't alter the fact of our oppression nor the imperative for change.

Amazement at our possible numbers, implied in the question, makes me feel like I'm in the zoo, and we are not talking about the human side of the fence. Like everywhere, in Melbourne we don't have any decent statistics but educated observations of gay men suggests that in the last five years our closets have almost emptied. It's possible that in Melbourne we are currently experiencing the largest population of free and out gay men that there has ever been in the history of mankind in this place. The 'free and out' part is more important to know than the actual numbers. Our proportion with respect to heterosexuals is irrelevant and focus on it is more likely to generate fear amongst homosexuals than progress.

Homosexuals have never ever been in this position before. For the first time in history we may be in a position to freely learn about ourselves and gain a heathy and confident understanding of where we are different to or the same as heterosexuals. For example, we might begin to understand fundamental things about the ways men might form relationships with each other. We might be able to create some functional community and cultural structures which are sorely needed at the moment.

Why are some women so attracted to dominant men?

23 October 2019

All humans have personalities. We might say that the extremes are dominant and submissive personalities. These two personality traits can complement each other when brought together. We can all think of couples where both are dominant, or both are submissive......it doesn't work very well. We are most likely to be attracted to the complementary personality because it will be comfortable for us.

How this plays out, though, is greatly influenced by history and culture (rather than nature). All men are encouraged to be dominant; all women are encouraged to be submissive. For some this can mean a struggle to meet expectations, or there is the battle to curb their natural personality.

Human society and culture have incorporated many features to ensure that gender linked personalities are achieved. The stereotype that we see is the dominant man and the submissive woman. While society tries to hide it, I'm sure you can think of examples of the dominant woman with a submissive male. And we say, 'he is under thumb' or 'we know who wears the pants in that household'.

What I have described is a natural, and partly man-made system trying to create productive unions. Other often strong forces, however, can result in the appearance of large amounts of disadvantage, abuse and violence in a society.

Is it likely the proportion of gay and lesbian people in the human population has been roughly constant for centuries?

7 May 2019

You pose what should be a simple question which in fact becomes exceedingly complex. What I write is not a criticism, but an opportunity to think about some of that complexity.

My answer will concentrate on gay men. It is likely that the story for lesbians is significantly different and I should not take away their voices.

With a question like this I'm afraid that terminology is very important. We are talking about something over centuries. It is important that we all know exactly what is being talked about. We should be cognisant of the impact of history on our communities, then and now. 'Gay' came into common use in about the late 1960s. Then it identified a culture rather than a sexuality. It has gradually come to identify sexuality and culture. The cultural part means that the word can't be used around the world, or indeed, across all generations within our own communities. I'm in Australia, it is in general use here, but not all around the world, which your question is considering.

Pre-gay lots of words were used. They were very regional, they came and went, they were street language. Almost all were derogatory. The word gay really helps us move on from that. For this question we should be using the word homosexual. Yes, it is medical, but its meaning is exact. All those other words can be translated into the word homosexual and we get some of the uniformity required for this sort of question. Although dating from the 1860s its use is almost timeless, as timeless as men having sex with each other. Whenever I am writing about history, at about 1960 I change my word from gay to homosexual. At that point it becomes more valid and useful and in itself reminds the audience of some very important history. I get criticised on Quora, seemingly our history didn't start until 1960! Personally, to this day I identify as homosexual, and my culture is gay.

We could now go through history and consider the many names about us that were being thrown around and try and determine if that name was actually connected with homosexuality. Then historical references using that name can become data. For it is data that is the big issue here. We have almost no statistical data other than police records for homosexual men. We still have great trouble understanding current population indices. Over the centuries, oppressive techniques have made homosexuals silent and invisible, effectively uncountable.

It is only with an educated consideration of the Biology underlying your question that we might guess that the proportions in the human population should not have changed. But homosexuals have a history of demonstrating unusual biology so we should make such conclusions with caution.

Who do we count? A bisexual man can often 'appear' to be homosexual depending on what he is doing at the time. In some countries, homosexual activities of certain cultural groups may be even more invisible or not understood at all. Society actively discouraged identification and counting. Remember the oppression wanted us to be invisible and silent. Many homosexual men didn't identify as homosexual, or even one of those words. They were just men having secret sex with another man in the park on Saturday night. How and who would have collected the data? Certainly not any government group. Researchers maybe, but they would never have received the funding, would they?

I pose another matter. I believe that at certain points of the oppression, like the 1950s in Australia, we were so invisible and so silent that we didn't even know who we were or that the option of sex in the park even existed. Key to our oppression is also making heterosexuals completely ignorant of us. I believe that countless men in these periods didn't even have the knowledge of what constituted homosexuality or what that meant to them. This is removal of the 'other'. They were neither heterosexual nor homosexual, they were just unhappy men destined to never even experience something core to their humanity. How do we count them? Are they really homosexual? Hard questions to answer, which could alter the proportions.

So the response to your question is just a best guess. The heterosexual world has centuries of data and research. They can draw conclusions and make decisions about now and the future using basic sociological information that we have only really started to get in some parts of the world since 2000. Think of the task we have. Newly liberated, but in only some parts of the world, largely damaged people, trying to create community, culture and be responsible for ourselves in the eyes of society........a tough task made all the harder without basic information about ourselves: who we are, how we think, how we have relationships, what sex looks like, and how many of us there are. So often the answers are very different for lesbians, the differences often a good example of the unusual biology I referred to earlier.

What we are seeing is just another example of where the aftermath of oppression can go on for generations because something as simple and useful as your question can't really be answered now.

In gay relationships, is one normally a Top and one a Bottom, or is it common to switch?

16 July 2019

You have forgotten Versatile. Tops and Bottoms don't usually change. It helps to get a match that facilitates a healthy sex life in a gay male relationship.

Some combinations work and some don't:
- Top with Top, not a match.
- Top with Versatile, some compromises needed.
- Versatile with Versatile, a perfect match.
- Versatile with Bottom, some compromises needed.
- Bottom with Bottom, not a match.
- Top with Bottom, a perfect match.

How can I become a better Top during gay sex?

7 July 2019

The difference between a good Top and an ok Top is the Top actually thinking about the Bottom. I aim to see if I can overload the Bottom with pleasure. He tries the same with me. We don't focus on ourselves, and there is an enormous pleasure exchange.

Skill: get to know the biology of a man's body. Skill never fails to excite and impress. Find out where it feels great for you and him. With vanilla sex, test things out and look for the response. Don't pound, do intimate, connected fucking. For that you need to be very hard and he can't be too tight. Mix up different fucking styles, look at his face as much as possible. Don't underestimate the power of holding inside which requires you to learn to resist thrusting.

Learn some kink, have a sort of menu. Make sure you learn kink from experts so you can do it effectively and safely. In chat when a Bottom asks what you are into, cut and paste your list, he will be impressed.

Role play and 'mind sex' can provide huge pleasures for a Top and Bottom. Not every Top is good at it but if you haven't already, develop roles and role play that turns you on. It's quite likely that it will turn on a Bottom as well.

You will find that everything will come together just that bit better with a Bottom of a similar height. Not that you shouldn't have adventures with guys of different sizes.

Stick to what you are good at and what you like. If you are a Top and you aren't interested in bottoming, then don't bottom. Put your energy into perfecting your topping. A Bottom will be pleased if you say to him, 'I'm a real Top I won't ask you to fuck me'. You both then focus on what you each do well.

What does it mean if a user on a gay dating site (Grindr or Planet Romeo) does not mention whether he's a Top/ Bottom/ Versatile? Is he someone who will change his sexual preference to hook-up? Is he not open or unsure about his sexual role?

29 June 2019

Yes, whether a guy is a Top, Bottom or Versatile makes a big difference to me as to whether I might approach the guy on the app. Bottoms are my clear preference.

If the profile doesn't indicate the role and there are plenty of guys in my area, then I usually just move onto the next profile. If there are not many guys around or if this guy is particularly interesting, then if chat ensues I will try and find out the guy's sex role fairly early in the chat. You've just got to ask it: 'are you Top, Bottom or Versatile?' Usually the guy replies.

You wonder why they didn't state it on their profile. Some possible reasons are:
- The guy is Versatile and thinks he can do everything and doesn't have to state his role.
- He is a Bottom. It's not fashionable to be a Bottom at the moment and they are not treated very well. The guy will look to see whether I am a Top, then he will say he is a Bottom.
- The guy is newly out and not sure.
- The guy thinks it is the most blatantly sexual information on the site and is prudish about it.
- The guy might be assuming there are links between the sex roles and the prevalence of STIs.

- The guy is very conservative in his views of dating and relationships and doesn't believe that sex should be mentioned so quickly.
- The guy is famous, wealthy or very beautiful and thinks he is above such discussions.

In terms of a guy changing his sexual preference to be able to hook-up, this is most likely to occur with a guy saying he is Versatile when he is really Top or Bottom. It's possible that he can get away it. It's less likely that a Versatile guy would say he is a Top because he is more likely to get caught out because he doesn't have the skill and can't maintain the erection required. A Versatile guy would definitely not say he is a Bottom because they usually think that Bottoms are scum.

What is the gay symbol for a passive partner or a Bottom partner?

5 May 2019

The words passive and active are really only used in the kink world where Bottom and Top don't really apply.

Generally speaking, a Top is active and a Bottom is passive. Notice that I used the nouns, they usually apply to the individuals and reference their whole role in sex. The verbs to top and to bottom just refer to the different roles in anal sex.

For historical reasons the words Top and Bottom don't serve us well. They would be much clearer if they were only used with Tops and Bottoms and never with Versatiles. After all, a Versatile guy who is bottoming is not a Bottom, he is a Versatile guy who is fucking. A Versatile guy is always a Versatile guy, he is never a Top and never a Bottom.

There is a lot of confusion and argument amongst gay men about this. I don't think your question can be answered until that settles.

When two gay men have anal sex, the Top is clearly erect. What about the Bottom?

26 April 2019

I'm a Top and I pretty well exclusively have sex with Bottoms. I can't speak for Versatile guys.

I rarely see a Bottom's penis erect. I think there are a number of factors.

A Bottom is innately less interested in his penis during sex than Versatile or Tops. His focus is his anus and he is less likely to be stimulating his penis.

My anal sex style may contribute. I don't pound with regular thrusts stimulating the prostate. I mix it up into connected sex. This has less prostate stimulation but more stimulation of other kinds.

The main cause as I see it is the prevalence of the use of recreational drugs with sex. It is known that the commonly used recreational drugs have the side effects of preventing an erection and delaying orgasm. This despite being otherwise aroused.

If you think about it, this would present a great problem for a Top but not a Bottom. I've been very active over the last 6 years and I might have seen 20 Bottoms reach orgasm during sex. That doesn't bother me though because I'm not interested in their penis.

What follows are comments that I received about my answer. I include them here as an example of the aggressive and nasty comments that have been coming from the UK.

Comment from XXX 28 February 2020.

"That doesn't bother me, I'm not interested in their penis." And then you feel upset when we call these two sexual roles a pathetic emulation of heterosexual sex roles, where one of you acts as a stunted straight-male wannabe, that claims to be into men, yet also claims not to be interested in the single most masculine thing about a man, his penis and his ability to use it, while the other is effectively castrated to the point that their penis becomes but a vestigial organ of some sorts and his ability to orgasm is dead and buried and whatever sexual 'pleasure' he may derive, meagre and pitiful as it may be, is derived by proxy.

This answer is a 'wonderful' example as to what happens to gay males when they internalise the homophobia, straight gender norms and the general ignorance they grow up in. Self-hate and self-mortification comes in many forms, some gay males hate being gay, others hate it so much they try to change, join ex-gay movements and undergo 'therapy', yet others force a 'straight lifestyle' upon themselves, marry females, have children and when they can't control themselves any more they fuck men in secret. And some morph their gender and sexual expression until it becomes nothing more than a parody of straight sex roles. A sad, tragic and often enough horrific parody, but parody nonetheless.

Whenever I read such a horrific testimony as to what self-hate does to a person in sexual terms, I am ever so grateful that the vast majority of gay males have not been afflicted in this manner. Most of us are happy with our masculinity intact, have no issues with being male and being attracted to other males, and have no desire to emulate heterosexual folk in any form or manner. The beauty of being gay and versatile is in the equality and sexual reciprocity that is at the core of our relationships, where both sides give and take, where both sides enjoy sex directly, and where both sides can express their masculinity and enjoy the other's ability to do the same.

The good news is that no one is born a so called 'top or bottom', these roles are anything but instinctual or inborn, and they emerge just like any other paraphilia, as a result of social influence and psychological imprinting. As such, countless individuals that were afflicted with this homophobic fixation emancipated themselves over the years. Hopefully one day soon our societies will be liberal and inclusive enough for gay males so that no young gay male ever has to feel like sacrificing a part of who they are in a futile and desperate attempt to be more like straight folk are.

Comment from PDS 28/2/2020:

Your comment bears little relevance to the question or my answer. It is written to offend and upset, not very productive. One really wonders what difference Tops and Bottoms make to your life such that we have to endure comments like this.

Comment from xxxx 7 March 2020

There is nothing I could say that could come even close to being as 'offensive' as the sexually crippling self-loathing you conjured up in your own answer. Nothing. In this department I'm afraid your only competition are other stunted homophobes that have internalised the homophobia around them just as efficiently as you have done.

Gay men can be referred to as twinks, bears, otters, etc. Does every gay man associate with one of these terms, or are the terms considered derogatory?

25 April 2019

It's interesting to ponder why gay men have so many subgroups and their names. While these names are not universally adopted by all gay men, they are by enough gay men. The rest will usually know about them and generally find them harmless, even amusing. This suggests they are a comfortable part of gay culture.

Male sexuality has a very physical focus. Usually it's the physicality of another man that draws us in first. If it gets to it, an interest in his mind and soul will follow. Having subgroup names (which usually connect with physical features) hones our taste, shortens the search, and increases the likelihood of success. They can also create supportive sub-communities which are valuable in difficult times.

There can be an element exclusivity. It's not common for straight people to know much about this at all. Where there has been such an adversarial history, a minority group is empowered by withholding aspects of their lives and culture from the oppressors.

Do gay Tops like to get fingered? He refuses to touch my dick and the important thing is he doesn't like to touch my butt with his hand (I'm very clean) and last night I was touching his butt and his dick got hard.

11 February 2019

I'm a Top. There are a lot of issues there, some probably not related to his sex role. I believe that most Tops don't gain great pleasure from their arse. Other things are more pleasurable. I don't believe that Tops like to be fingered. Usually the opposite is true.

A proportion of Tops will suck every dick, some will sometimes suck a dick, and there is a group who don't suck any dick. Why it's like this I don't know. I'm in the middle group. I wouldn't read too much into the fact that he didn't touch your dick. This is not uncommon for a Top.

That he doesn't like touching your arse is unusual. Tops love getting their fingers, hands, cock, fists, indeed anything in there. It's probably not your arse that's the problem, he probably has some sort of OCD about cleanliness.

That you touched his arse and he got hard probably demonstrates that some Tops can be anally stimulated or that he is really Versatile or Bottom.

Our community has been treated pretty poorly by society. So many men are quite screwed up about sex. We have to expect some strange behaviours.

Does population density affect sexuality?

10 February 2019

Speaking about gay men, the population density in a given place has been a key determinant in the coming out of gay men, the development of a gay community and the progress of gay rights. It can greatly increase the number of people identifying as a certain sexuality.

A higher density of gay men can mean that a critical mass can be reached where what are a minority are able to overcome the influence of the majority.

My boyfriend is strictly Top. Should I worry over our relationship if he's willing to switch role but doesn't feel comfortable as a Bottom?

22 January 2019

I think the important thing is that you are both comfortable with what is happening. The worst thing would be if one of you felt obliged to flip or change roles when you didn't really want to. If you think about it, it's harder for the Top to change than for the Bottom. Tops and Bottoms should be respected over this issue. You should reject any pressure you receive from outside the relationship.

I'm single now but I probably change sides once per year. I don't desire to take it up the arse (that's a key sign of a Top), but I do it for other reasons (I'm hopeless at it anyway). Maybe I want to see what something feels like from the Bottom's perspective. It might be a gift for the bottom (where he wants to give it as well), or with a fully Versatile guy because they give the best beginners anal sex and it's good training for me to watch. Once per year doesn't make me Top Vers. I'm still a total Top. The word 'desire' helps you work that out.

Is it more enjoyable to be Top or Bottom in gay sex?

25 December 2018

There is no one answer, it depends on the guy.

Firstly, your question has an error. There are actually three sex positions in gay sex: Top, Bottom, Versatile. We should consider all three if we are to get a clear picture.

Each gay man is sort of coded as to which sex position he likes. This is via the instinctual erotic drivers of dominance and submission. Those that only have dominance will desire to be a Top. Those that only have submission will desire to be a Bottom. Those that have a mixture of dominance and submission will desire to be Versatile and enjoy both Bottom and Top style sex.

For each individual there will be one sex position that is more enjoyable than the others. Of course, we can override these instinctual desires and engage in any type of gay sex, but the desires don't go away and ultimately, we are happiest when we follow them.

In a gay/lesbian relationship how do you decide who's the dominant and who's the passive partner?

21 December 2018

I can only speak for gay male relationships. Our personalities can influence the way we interact with the world. Some personalities tend to be more dominant and some more passive. This can come out in the way the individuals behave in the relationship. But it's no given that there will be one of these dominant personalities and one of the passive personalities present in the relationship, or even that they are stereotypical. Other combinations occur. It's important not to ascribe gender differences to this as well.

As far as sexual personalities go, the presence of dominant and passive roles in the relationship can be more clear-cut. It is important, however, to acknowledge that unlike heterosexual sex there are three sex roles in gay sex; Top, Versatile and Bottom. Each should be considered.

Versatile sex is essentially democratic. Dominance and passivity pay only small parts in the erotic environment and even then, it changes as the participants flip.

Top/Bottom sex, however, is quite dependent on dominance and passivity (actually submission) for the sex to work. For Tops and Bottoms deciding whether they are dominant or passive is quite easy. The desires for one or the other are quite strong and obvious. These men have no tendency towards Versatility, so they also get a clue by observing the role that they have no desire for.

We really need to remember that not everything is binary.

For gay men who say you're a Top only, would you ever let your Versatile boyfriend Top you, as he has needs you're not fulfilling?

2 December 2018

I'm a Top.

Firstly, the chances are not high that I would have a Versatile boyfriend. The most ideal would be for my boyfriend to be my sexual match, which is a Bottom.

I am fucked from time to time. I don't really get any pleasure from my arse so when I am fucked it's usually for other reasons. Maybe it's a gift of my vulnerability to the other guy, or maybe it is an experiment and I am trying to understand some aspect of the arse. It takes a lot of effort on my part and I'll always be a baby fuck.

Gay men are very good at doing open relationships. In the case you describe the boyfriend would identify up front his needs and I would certainly agree to an open relationship where he could satisfy his desire to fuck, outside of the relationship. This is common sense between two adults. Much better than letting the difference gnaw away at the relationship.

Equally, I would be permitted to go outside of the relationship to satisfy my desire to be a Top with a Bottom. Versatile guys restrict themselves from experiencing the full range of male on male sex in that they don't initiate or participate in sexual role play and the mind sex that goes on between Tops and Bottoms. This second layer of sex (the first being sex of the activities) that Tops and Bottoms enjoy is intense, satisfying and ignored by Versatile guys. I can only enjoy it with a Bottom.

Where do you think sex and sexuality are headed in the near future after observing current trends?

1 December 2018

I'm answering as a gay man in Australia.

For the first time in human history we have such a large and complete (age, looks, ethnicity, culture) population of gay men who are out and visible. This is an enormous change from even 15 years ago. We are largely free.

Our recorded history is very fragmented, there has been little research done on us, we are a population of damaged men from our earlier experiences. In the major cities we have reached a critical mass in certain areas that we can now develop a wholistic culture, including a sex culture.

The straight community thinks they have done their job. Part of being free is we stop the double life, stop the endless work to fit in. But now we are finding just that, we are ourselves, but we don't fit in. We don't yet have a culture to support us in that or to even challenge the straight culture. So the dislocation continues.

Here the formation of culture is going through a dangerous phase. Most gay men don't know what's going on. After a lifetime of being told what to be, they are suspicious of a gay culture that might do the same. There is a lot of drug fuelled experimentation in sex happening. It's a shaky time. We have no leaders to steer the course. Few thinkers providing ideas.

We are doing an almost impossible job with meagre tools. There should be recognition that gay men suffered under systemic oppression for decades with effects that will be long lasting. Society at large is responsible and should do something. There should be investigation of how the effects of the oppression are lingering. We should get assistance in forming culture, for it is culture that will bring stability to the community. In the past the oppression denied us the ability to form culture. This needs to happen as a matter of urgency.

What follows is an example of a completely dead pan answer to an outrageous question.

If people were detected as gay in utero, should those people be aborted?

3 November 2018

Certainly, that could be done with reliable detection in utero within the time frame for safe abortion. Many human attributes could be dealt with this way, as long as the testing is there and is reliable.

In terms of eliminating homosexuals from a family it could be quite effective. The program would have to continue into the future with every pregnancy in the family being checked. Assuming the women in the family comply, a family could be homosexual-free forever if the program doesn't stop. There is always the possibility of a testing error producing a homosexual, a contingency plan would be needed to eliminate that person once the sexuality is confirmed.

To eliminate homosexuals from a whole society, referred to as genocide, would take much more effort. Every pregnancy would have to be tested. Compliance would be difficult as many would not support the move. With such large numbers the reliability of the testing would really come under the limelight as a false negative means a homosexual is not aborted and a false positive means a heterosexual (or other) is aborted. You can imagine the repercussions of that.

Total genocide or extermination would be very difficult because:
- The limitations of the testing.
- Compliance by the Women.
- The law not applying to the whole world, with some leakage of homosexuals back into the population.

- Homosexuals are constantly being born from heterosexuals. The program would have to be relentless if total extermination is the aim.
- The best time for this may have been 80–100 years ago. But the technology wasn't there.

We may get the technology, but I'm confident to say that you will never get the people's support on this one. Fortunately, we do seem to have some collective moral lines that aren't crossed.

How and why do some gay men become Versatile?

16 October 2018

They don't become Versatile, they are Versatile. Society's pressures on gay men does mean that sometimes they were not able to be true to their natural sexual role.

The concept of Top and Bottom was probably invented in the 1960s to help gay men quickly work things out with anal sex. We used the heterosexual model. Unfortunately, we didn't notice that Versatile men were different. In terms of anal sex on its own, at any point in time they may look like a Bottom or a Top. The heterosexual model didn't help because there is no versatility in heterosexual sex.

What we have seen in recent years is a large movement of gay men out of the Top and Bottom roles and into the Versatile role where they always belonged.

Do the gay concepts of "Top" and "Bottom" roughly line up with traditional male and female roles in a relationship?

14 October 2018

No, Top and Bottom refer to sex roles in gay relationships. They rarely impact on the general role of two men in a relationship, so do not correlate with male and female roles in a relationship.

The words Top and Bottom were probably adopted by gay men in the 1960s. They specifically referred to anal sex. If you think about it, it's not immediately obvious which man would be the penetrator and which the receptor. Using one of those words would allow the situation to be understood quite quickly and easily at an encounter in a park, which was probably where much sex between men happened. Having sex in a bed in a house with the light on was a later revolution for gay men.

Only two words were created, it was binary, and in this aspect matched up with the binary nature of heterosexual sex.

Several decades later we realised we had made a mistake. With sex between two men there is a third group, the Versatiles. Men who desire and participate in anal sex as both the penetrator and receptor. We didn't notice it earlier because at any point in time a Versatile guy might look like a Top or Bottom and we didn't have a cohesive community where flipping could be seen over the long term rather than just a fleeting encounter.

The second reason we missed it is very interesting. When we looked at heterosexual sex and confirmed its binary nature, we didn't realise that there cannot be versatility in heterosexual sex. We should have had three words not two.

Recent data from Melbourne in Australia shows that approximately 15% of gay men identify as Top, approximately 15% as Bottom, and 70% as Versatile. The Versatile group is now dominant.

The words have also become more sophisticated. They still refer to the position in anal sex but increasingly they refer to other sexual features of the individuals adopting the word. For example, a Bottom would desire to be submissive, have receptive oral sex, and the subordinate role in much kink. The Top would desire to be dominant, may not do anything with the Bottom's penis, and be the dominant in kink. Versatile guys can desire to do everything. The words can refer to the wholistic and desired (natural) behaviour and role of the individual in male to male sex. Increasingly we find that an individual has natural desires and behaviours that align them with one of the three words. They can guide us in understanding how the individual wants to have sex. While a guy might learn to perform sexual activities normally associated with one of the other groups, it won't come naturally to him. He cannot change the underlying desire. I believe that we will find the three groups continue and there won't be much movement between them. Gay men will naturally align with one group and discover the sex that is most satisfying for them.

Of course this wasn't really studied in the past, when homosexuality was illegal. Since becoming freer, we are only now developing a sex culture which might help us and guide young gay men in what has become a complex system completely foreign to the heterosexual world. Clearly the heterosexual sex culture doesn't help us. Gay sex is moving further away from any heterosexual comparator. Adding the Versatile group to your question would now pose some difficulty.

My friends frequently like to poke fun at me for being a gay Bottom, should I care?

12 October 2018

Yes you should. If your friends are not queer, then they really should not be discussing your private sexual role.

If they are your gay friends, then it's not productive at all. Bottoms generally have a hard time in gay sexual culture. When a group is having a hard time that's exactly when you don't make fun of them.

In addition, Bottoms' natural sexual behaviour is submission. It's a highly erotic state for them. In gay sex terms they are more vulnerable and less equipped to assert or defend themselves. We should not take advantage of that.

Why are most gay men Bottoms? Most will say Versatile, but in reality they wind up almost always Bottoming. Even the Tops want to Bottom.

20 September 2018

We need to be clear on the terminology. Current usage seems to be that the verbs, to bottom and to top, refer to anal sex only. A Bottom, a Top and a Versatile, refer to gay men and the influence of domination/submission on the type of sex they desire. It's much more than about anal sex.

The desire to bottom varies from very strong in a Bottom, to negligible in a Top. Versatile guys vary in between. So essentially a Bottom likes to bottom, a Bottom Vers likes to bottom, Versatile guys like to bottom, and even Top Vers guys like to bottom sometimes. Only Tops seldom ever bottom.

Probably 15% of gay men might be Bottoms. A similar number are Tops. Probably 70% of gay men are Versatile. They like to bottom too, that's part of being Versatile.

But a Versatile man is never a Bottom. A Versatile man is never a Top. A Versatile man is always a Versatile man no matter what he is doing.

What is the largest population in the world of gay men: Tops, Bottoms or Versatile? Why?

19 July 2018

This is a very difficult question. The population we are speaking of, gay men, has suffered, and in some parts of the world still does suffer, from decades of oppression. This has resulted in many gay men experiencing damaging lives. As male to male penetrative anal sex is at the core of the oppression, then it's not surprising that a lot of us might be a bit mixed up about sex.

Gay sex and gay culture are still forming. We are still discovering things about ourselves that had long been hidden in the oppression. Speaking from Melbourne in Australia, we have in recent years had an explosion in the number of gay men identifying as Versatile in sex. 25 years ago Versatile gay men barely existed. These men, formerly counted in the ranks of Bottom or Top, were never happy there. The formation of the Versatile group has meant huge shifts of men between Top, Versatile, Bottom, etc. I have been keeping an eye on numbers, using the most popular gay app in Melbourne. Not highly scientific, but the numbers are different enough to be significant. Approximately 80% identify as Versatile (incl. Bottom Vers and Top Vers). About 10% each for Bottom and Top.

I use those words as nouns, they indicate a wholistic sexual picture, not just anal sex. The verbs, to bottom or to top are used more specifically to indicate anal sex. I believe that the numbers I give are also supported by biology. Dominance and submission are powerful forces all influencing human sex not just gay. We each get some or both of these forces from nature. As always there is a scale from 100% dominance through a grey scale with a mixed presentation, to 100% submission. These forces greatly influence our desires and the sex we have. 100% dominance is a Top, there's no versatility in 100% dominance. 100% submission is a Bottom, equally versatile-free. The grey scale includes the Versatile guys who benefit to varying degrees from both the dominance and submission forces in their sex, and they can flip from one to the other. This equips them with the all-important desires to engage in all roles and activities. The desire of Tops and Bottoms is fixed. Sure, humans have free will and can override the desire, but they cannot change the desire. We all want to be where our desires take us.

I think it will take some time for this to flesh out around the world, for gay culture to provide structure, and for a population of largely damaged men to finally follow their desires.

Further Reading

Adriaens, P. R., & De Block, A. (2006). The evolution of a social construction: the case of male homosexuality. *Perspectives in Biology and Medicine, 49*(4), 570-585.

Alice. (13 June 2018). Not all gay men have anal sex. Blog: *Go Ask Alice!.* http://goaskalice.columbia.edu, Retrieved 23 September 2018.

Ayres, I., & Leudeman, R. (2013). Tops, bottoms, and versatiles: What straight views of penetrative preferences could mean for sexuality claims under Price Waterhouse. *The Yale Law Journal, 123*(3), 714-768.

Bancroft, J. (2009). *Human sexuality and its problems* (3rd edition). Edinburgh, United Kingdom: Churchill Livingston.

Barker, M. J. (2018). *The psychology of sex*. Abigdon, United Kingdom: Routledge.

Bailey, J. M., Kim, P. Y., Hills, A., & Linsenmeier, J. A. W. (1997). Butch, femme, or straight acting? Partner preferences of gay men and lesbians. *Journal of Personality and Social Psychology, 73*(5), 960-973.

Belcourt, B., Dust, G., & Gabriel, K. (10 October 2018). Top or bottom: How do we desire? *The New Inquiry* online. Retrieved from: https://thenewinquiry.com/top_or_bottom_how_do_we_desire/.

The Rise of the Versatile

Bering, J. (16 September 2009). Top scientists get to the bottom of gay male sex role preferences. Scientific American Blog: *Bering in Mind*. Retrieved from: https://blogs.scientificamerican.com/bering-in-mind/top-scientists-get-to-the-bottom-of-gay-male-sex-role-preferences/.

Brennan, J. (2018). Size matters: Penis size and sexual position in gay porn profiles. *Journal of Homosexuality, 65*(7), 912-933.

Brooks, T. R., Reysen, S., & Shaw, J. (2017). Smashing back doors in: Negative attitudes toward bottoms within the gay community. *World Journal of Social Science Research 4*(2), 129-139.

Carrier, J. (1977). Sex-role preference as an explanatory variable in homosexual behaviour. *Archives of Sexual Behavior, 6*(1), 53-65.

Carter, E. R. A. (2015). Who's on top? The mental health of men who have sex with men. *Inquiry: The University of Arkansas Undergraduate Research Journal, 18*, article 5, 4-15.

Dangerfield, D. T., Laramie, R. S., Williams, J., Unger, J., & Bluthenthal, R. (2017). Sexual positioning among men who have sex with men: a narrative review. *Archives of Sexual Behavior, 46*(4), 869-884.

Dempsey, M. J. (updated 18 May 2016). Gay Men and Bottom Shaming (VIDEO, 3 min 48 sec). *HuffPost*, on-line. Retrieved from: https://www.huffpost.com/entry/gay-men-bottom-shaming_b_7288252.

Diamond, J. (2015). *Why is sex fun? The evolution of human sexuality* (2nd ed.). London, England: Weidenfeld & Nicolson.

Di Sciascio, P. (14 September 2018). Defining gay male sex roles [Blog post]. *Little Gay Blog*. Retrieved from: http://littlegayblog.com/gay-male-sex-roles.

The Rise of the Versatile

Donaghue, C. (2015). *Sex outside the lines: authentic sexuality in a sexually dysfunctional culture*. Dallas, Tx: BenBella Books.

Easton, D., & Hardy, J. W. (2001). *The new bottoming book* (2nd ed.). Gardena, CA: Greenery Press.

Easton, D., & Hardy, J. W. (2003). *The new topping book* (2nd ed.). Gardena, CA: Greenery Press.

Geddes, P., & Thompson, J. A. (2019). *The evolution of sex*. (n.p.): Alpha Editions. (Original work published 1889).

Gil, S. (2007). A Narrative exploration of gay men's sexual practices as a dialectical dialogue. *Sexual and Relationship Therapy, 22*(1), 63-75.

Gray, P. B., & Garcia, J. R. (2013). *Evolution & human sexual behavior*. Cambridge, MA: Harvard University Press.

Hancock, J. (24 March 2017). What does top and bottom mean? *Bishuk* online. Retrieved from: https://www.bishuk.com/sex/top-bottom-mean/.

Harry, J., & DeVall, W. B. (1978). *The social organization of gay males*. New York, NY: Praeger.

Hart, T. A., Wolitski, R. J., Purcell, D. W., Gomez, C., Halkitis, P., & The Seropositive Urban Men's Study Team. (2003). Sexual behavior among HIV-positive men who have sex with men: What's in a label? *The Journal of Sex Research, 40*(2), 179-188.

Henderson, N. J. (2018). 'Top, bottom, versatile': Narratives of sexual practices in gay relationships in the Cape Metropole, South Africa. *Culture, Health & Sexuality, 20*(11), 1145-1156.

Hoang, T. H. (2014). *A view from the bottom: Asian American masculinity and sexual representation*. London, UK: Duke University Press.

The Rise of the Versatile

Hoppe, T. (2011). Circuits of power, circuits of pleasure: Sexual scripting in gay men's bottom narratives. *Sexualities, 14*(2), 193-217.

Johns, M. J., Pingel, E., Eisenberg, A., Santana, M. L., & Bauermeister, J. (2012). "Butch tops and femme bottoms"?: Sexual roles, sexual decision-making, and ideas of gender among young gay men. *American Journal of Men's Health, 6*(6), 505-518.

Jozifkova, E., & Flegr, J. (2006). Dominance, submissivity (and homosexuality) in general population. Testing of evolutionary hypothesis of sadomasochism by internet-trap-method. *Neuroendocrinology Letters, 27*(6), 711-718.

Jozifkova, E., & Konvicka, M. (2009). Sexual arousal by higher- and lower-ranking partner: Manifestation of a mating strategy? *Journal of Sexual Medicine, 6*(12), 3327-3334.

Jozifkova, E., Konvicka, M., & Flegr, J. (2014). Why do some women prefer submissive men? Hierarchically disparate couples reach higher reproductive success in European urban humans. *Neuroendocrinology Letters, 35*(7), 594-601.

Jozifkova, E., & Kolackova, M. (2017). Sexual arousal by dominance and submission in relation to increased reproductive success in the general population. *Neuroendocrinology Letters, 38*(5), 381-387.

Juzwiak, R. (3 March 2015). Who's the man? How being versatile in bed is a way of life. *Gawker*, online. Retrieved from: https://gawker.com/whos-the-man-how-being-versatile-in-bed-is-a-way-of-li-1684296567.

Juzwiak, R. (28 April 2017). Born to bottom? Researchers report biological correlations in anal sex role in gay men. *Jezebel*, online. Retrieved from: https://jezebel.com/born-to-bottom-researchers-report-biological-correlati-1794233584.

The Rise of the Versatile

Kagan, D. (11 November 2015). Butt politics: The complexities of anal sex. *Archer Magazine #5*, unpaginated. ISSN: 2204-7352.

Kheraj, A. (7 June 2018). It's time to take your temperature on topping and bottoming. *GQ*, online. Retrieved from: https://www.gq.com/story/its-time-to-take-your-temperature-on-topping-and-bottoming.

Kheraj, A. (28 June 2018). The biggest myth about gay sex: Penetration isn't everything. *GQ*, online. Retrieved from: https://www.gq.com/story/the-biggest-myth-about-gay-sex.

Kiguwa, P., & Nduna, M. (2017). Top or bottom? Varsity youth talk about gay sexuality in a Stepping Stones workshop: Implications for sexual health. *South African Journal of Higher Education, 31*(4), 150-166.

Kippax, S. & Smith, G. (2001). Anal intercourse and power in sex between men. *Sexualities, 4*(4), 413-434.

Kort, J. (updated 2 February 2016). Guys on the 'side': Looking beyond gay tops and bottoms. *HuffPost*, online. Retrieved from: https://www.huffpost.com/entry/guys-on-the-side-looking-beyond-gay-tops-and-bottoms_b_3082484.

Kowalski, J. A. (2016). Sex-partner roles in homoerotic relations: An attempt of classification, *Journal of Homosexuality, 63*(1), 87-102.

Sondheim, S. (1959). *Let Me Entertain You* [lyrics]. Lyrics.com. Retrieved February 26, 2020, from https://www.lyrics.com/lyric/6053327/Sandra+Church.

Lick, D. J., & Johnson, K. L. (2015). Intersecting race and gender cues are associated with perceptions of gay men's preferred sexual roles. *Archives of Sexual Behavior, 44*(5), 1471-1481.

The Rise of the Versatile

McGill, C. M., & Collins J. C. (2014). *The experience of "Bottoming": considerations for identity and learning.* Conference proceedings paper presented at the South Florida Education Conference (8-23), Florida International University, Miami, USA, 7 June 2014.

Morin, J. (2010). *Anal pleasure & health; A guide for men, women and couples* (4th revised edition). (n.p.): Down There Press.

Moskowitz, D. A., Rieger, G., & Roloff, M. E. (2008). Tops, bottoms and versatiles. *Sexual and Relationship Therapy, 23*(3), 191-202.

Moskowitz, D. A., & Hart, T. A. (2011). The influence of physical body traits and masculinity on anal sex roles in gay and bisexual men. *Archives of Sexual Behavior, 40*(4), 835-841.

Moskowitz, D. A., & Roloff, M. E. (2017). Recognition and construction of top, bottom, and versatile orientations in gay/bisexual men. *Archives of Sexual Behavior, 46*(1), 273-283.

Moskowitz, D. A., & Garcia, C. P. (2019). Top, bottom and versatile anal sex roles in same-sex male relationships: Implications for relationship and sexual satisfaction. *Archives of Sexual Behavior, 48*(4), 1217-1225.

Moylan, B. (10 November 2016). Why are gay guys convinced the world is full of bottoms? *Vice*, online. Retrieved from: https://www.vice.com/en_us/article/jmkjx4/why-are-gay-guys-convinced-the-world-is-full-of-bottoms.

Ogas, O., & Gaddam, S. (2011). *A billion wicked thoughts: What the world's largest experiment reveals about human desire.* New York, NY: Penguin Group (USA) Inc.

Phoenix, K. (2014). *Special report #2: Why tops don't care, why the bottoms are crazy and why the versatiles lie.* New York, NY: The Omni Group, Inc.

The Rise of the Versatile

Pachankis, J. E., Buttenwieser, I. G., Bernstein L. B., & Bayles, D. O. (2013). A longitudinal, mixed methods study of sexual position identity, behaviour, and fantasies among young sexual minority men. *Archives of Sexual Behavior, 42*(7), 1241-1253.

Queer Voices. (updated 2 February 2016). Gay 'top' and 'bottom' roles generalized by stereotypes, Archives of Sexual Behavior study finds. *HuffPost*, online. Retrieved from: http://www.huffingtonpost.com/2013/04/08/gay-top-and-bottom-study_n_3038492.html.

Ravenhill, J. P., & de Visser, R. O. (2017). Perceptions of gay men's masculinity are associated with their sexual self-label, voice quality and physique. *Psychology & Sexuality, 8*(3), 208-222.

Ravenhill, J, P., & de Visser, R. O. (2018). "It takes a man to put me on the bottom": Gay men's experiences of masculinity and anal intercourse. *Journal of Sex Research, 55*(8), 1033-1047.

Reilly, R. (2016). Top or bottom: a position paper. *Psychology & Sexuality, 7*(3), 167-176.

Ryan, C., & Jetha, C. (2011). *Sex at dawn: The prehistoric origins of modern sexuality* (2nd ed.). Brunswick, Australia: Scribe Publications.

Scholz, M. S., Damm, O., Elkenkamp, S., Marcus, U., Greiner, W., & Schmidt, A. J. (2019). Population size and self-reported characteristics and sexual preferences of men-who-have-sex-with-men (MSM) in Germany based on social network data. *PloS One, 14*(2), e0212175.

Selzer, L. F. (11 June 2012). Dominant or submissive? Paradox of power in sexual relations. *Psychology Today*, online. Retrieved from: https://www.psychologytoday.com/au/blog/evolution-the-self/201206/dominant-or-submissive-paradox-power-in-sexual-relations.

The Rise of the Versatile

Selzer, L. F. (6 June 2012). Gay or straight, a male is a male is a male. *Psychology Today*, online. Retrieved from: https://www.psychologytoday.com/au/blog/evolution-the-self/201206/gay-or-straight-male-is-male-is-male.

Selzer, L. F. (25 May 2012). You can't much help what turns you on. *Psychology Today*, online. Retrieved from: https://www.psychologytoday.com/au/blog/evolution-the-self/201205/you-can-t-much-help-what-turns-you.

Selzer, L. F. (17 May 2012). Paradox and pragmatism in women's sexual desire. *Psychology Today*, online. Retrieved from: https://www.psychologytoday.com/au/blog/evolution-the-self/201205/paradox-and-pragmatism-in-women-s-sexual-desire.

Selzer, L. F. (14 May 2012). The triggers of sexual desire pt 2: What's erotic for women? *Psychology Today*, online. Retrieved from: https://www.psychologytoday.com/au/blog/evolution-the-self/201205/the-triggers-sexual-desire-pt-2-what-s-erotic-women.

Selzer, L. F. (11 May 2012). The triggers of sexual desire: men vs. women. *Psychology Today*, online. Retrieved from: https://www.psychologytoday.com/au/blog/evolution-the-self/201205/the-triggers-sexual-desire-men-vs-women.

Seriously Science. (6 November 2013). Gay men's preferences for "top" vs. "bottom" can be judged by their face. *Discover Magazine*, online. Retrieved from: https://www.discovermagazine.com/mind/gay-mens-preferences-for-top-vs-bottom-can-be-judged-by-their-face.

Shaw, L., Wang, L., Cui, Z., Rich, A. J., Armstrong, H. L., Lachowsky, N. J., & Roth, E. A. (2019). Longitudinal event-level analysis of gay and bisexual men's anal sex versatility: Behavior, roles and substance use. *Journal of Sex Research, 56*(9), 1136-1146.

The Rise of the Versatile

Silverstein, C., & Picano, Felice. (1992). *The new joy of gay sex* (1st edition). New York, NY: Harper Collins.

Simes, G. (1992). The Language of Homosexuality in Australia, in *Gay Perspectives: Essays in Australian Gay Culture.* Aldrich, R., & Wotherspoon, G. (Eds.). Sydney, Australia: Department of Economic History, The University of Sydney.

Slide, A. (2015). *Gay's the word: being a brief history of the secret language of homosexuality.* Albany, Ga: BearManor Bear.

Sohn, A. (22 May 2003). Who's on top?, *New York Magazine.* Retrieved from:
http://nymag.com/nymetro/nightlife/sex/columns/nakedcity/n_872 8/.

Taywaditep, K. J. (2002). Marginalization among the marginalized: Gay men's anti-effeminacy attitudes. *Journal of Homosexuality, 42*(1), 1-28.

Tieu, H. V., Li, X., Donnell, D., Vittinghoff, E., Buchbinder, S., Parente, Z. G., & Koblin, B. (2013). Anal sex role segregation and versatility among men who have sex with men: EXPLORE study. *Journal of Acquired Immune Deficiency Syndrome, 64*(1), 121-125.

"Top/Bottom". *Encyclopedia of Sex and Gender: Culture Society History.* Retrieved February 25, 2020 from Encyclopedia.com: https://www.encyclopedia.com/social-sciences/encyclopedias-almanacs-transcripts-and-maps/topbottom.

Tskhay, K. O., & Rule, N. O. (2013). Accurate identification of a preference for insertive versus receptive intercourse from static facial cues of gay men. *Archives of Sexual Behavior, 42*(7), 1217-1222.

Underwood, S. G. (2003). *Gay men and anal eroticism: tops, bottoms, and versatiles.* Binghampton, NY: The Howarth Press, Inc.

The Rise of the Versatile

Wegesin, D. J., & Meyer-Bahlburg, H. F. L. (2000). Top/bottom self-label, anal sex practices, HIV risk and gender role identity in gay men in New York City. *Journal of Psychology & Human Sexuality, 12*(3), 43-62.

Wei, C., & Raymond, H. F. (2011). Preference for and maintenance of anal sex roles among men who have sex with men: sociodemographic and behavioural correlates. *Archives of Sexual Behavior, 40*(4), 829-834.

Wikipedia Contributors. (2018). *Focus on: Male homosexuality* (Kindle Edition). OK Publishing. Retrieved from: https://www.amazon.com.au/Focus-Homosexuality-Practices-Handkerchief-Pornography-ebook/dp/B07DY478F9/ref=sr_1_1?keywords=focus+on+male+homosexuality&qid=1580295454&s=digital-text&sr=1-1.

Wong, B. (updated 9 June 2019). Everything you wanted to know about tops and bottoms. *Huffington Post*, online. Retrieved from https://www.huffingtonpost.com.au/entry/tops-and-bottoms-in-gay-sex_l_5cf58f6ee4b0e8085e3ec6aa.

Yee, N. (2002). *Beyond tops and bottoms: Correlations between sex-role preference and physical preferences for partners among gay men.* Retrieved from: http://www.nickyee.com/ponder/topbottom.html.

Yee, N. (2003). *Catching the phoenix: The social construction of homosexuality.* Retrieved from: http://www.nickyee.com/ponder/social_construction.html.

Zheng, L., Hart, T. A., & Zheng, Y. (2012). The relationship between intercourse preference positions and personality traits among gay men in China. *Archives of Sexual Behavior, 41*(3), 683-689.

Zheng, L., Hart, T. A., & Zheng, Y. (2015). Top/bottom sexual self-labels and empathizing-systemizing cognitive styles among gay men in China. *Archives of Sexual Behavior, 44*(5), 1431-1438.

The Rise of the Versatile

Zheng, L. (2019). The dyadic effects of top/bottom sexual self-labels and partner sexual role requirements on facial masculinity preferences among gay and bisexual men in China. *The Journal of Sex Research*. Advance online publication. doi: 10.1080/00224499.2019.1680596.

www.ingramcontent.com/pod-product-compliance
Lightning Source LLC
Chambersburg PA
CBHW020708270326
41928CB00005B/323